Praise for *F*ck Like a Goddess*

"Sharp, forceful debut . . . While Roxo's shrewd strategies are tailored for women, anyone eager for more intrepidness in their self-improvement will find dynamic strategies here."

—PUBLISHERS WEEKLY

"Come for the meditation coaching, stay to get in touch with the divine feminine within."

—MARISA MELTZER, *New York Times* columnist

"Alexandra writes from the rawness of her heart and experience. Her gift is in liberating those around her by embodying her truth in every moment."

—LINDSEY SIMCIK and KRISTA WILLIAMS, *Almost 30* podcast

"Simply being around Roxo's exhilarating, vivacious presence is a revitalizing retreat in and of itself."

—KARA LADD, lifestyle partnerships editor, *Harper's Bazaar*

"Alexandra Roxo is a true visionary. With this book, she is helping women everywhere to heal from the sexual trauma, body hatred, and distorted self-image that insidiously keep so many of us playing small. Rooted in the deeply personal process of facing and integrating her own demons, Alexandra's commitment to fearlessly walking her own talk is testament to her integrity as a spiritual leader for the now age."

—RUBY WARRINGTON, author of *Material Girl, Mystical World* and *Sober Curious*

"If you are ready to burst into a life where your body, sexuality, and voice are considered sacred, then devour the pages of *F*ck Like a Goddess.*"

—SAHARA ROSE, author of *Eat Feel Fresh* and host of the *Highest Self Podcast*

"In her new book, Alexandra Roxo reminds us of our feminine power and that sensuality and devotion belong together."

—REBECCA CAMPBELL, bestselling author of *Rise Sister Rise* and *Light Is the New Black*

"I am a huge fan of Alexandra, both as a friend and colleague, and I am absolutely overjoyed to celebrate the success of her book! She is an utterly amazing teacher with a powerful and clear methodology that elicits serious results. Her insights and energy are an incredibly potent source of inspiration and healing to women. *F*ck Like a Goddess* is a stunning distillation of Alexandra's mission, overflowing with loving and invaluable wisdom to help women unlock their potential to overcome their boundaries and explore a more limitless feminine existence. It is a must-read!"

—SAH D'SIMONE, meditation and spiritual teacher and author of *5-Minute Daily Meditations*

"Alexandra takes you there. She walks with you. She talks to *you*. She's not afraid of the shadow and in integrating it brings more light to life. Her stories, her courage, and her voice resonating in every part of my body. Gratitude to her for walking her path and illuminating a path for so many women. Simple truths, clarity, and brave beauty make up her work and this book. Thank you, Alexandra."

—LISA LEVINE, founder of *Maha Rose*

"In this book, Alexandra guides us in embracing sacred practices that have been used for millennia to help us live our most embodied lives. Through ritual, breathwork, sex magick, and storytelling, Alexandra weaves a web of divine magick, guiding us back into our fullest potential of living in a state of presence and pure love. This book is written with so much tender care and compassion, while still being enticing and exciting. By using her own stories and experiences, Alexandra is able to effortlessly show us the path back to our truth, our freedom, and our sensual and delicious depths."

—GABRIELA HERSTIK, author of *Bewitching the Elements* and *Inner Witch*

"If this book calls to you, it's because you've been hiding and your soul knows you have BIG work to do in this world. If you're ready to stop letting opinions or fear hold you back and unleash the most powerful version of you, apply what this book says to your life."

—LORI HARDER, author of *A Tribe Called Bliss*

"If you are ready to transform your relationship to your body, FINALLY find your joy, supercharge your confidence, and renew your connection to the Divine Feminine power you absolutely have inside you, you have to read this book. Alexandra Roxo has written a fiery, fiercely honest manifesto on self-love unlike anything else on the market. This is a real-as-f*ck guidebook on womanhood that welcomes ALL women into the conversation. A radical, positive, planetary shift fueled by unapologetic self-acceptance is embarking onto the next generation of women, and Roxo is leading the charge."

—JESSICA ZWEIG, CEO and founder of SimplyBe

"Juicy spirituality! The ultimate read for those ready to step into their whole damn self. I can imagine Lizzo has this on her nightstand."

—EMMA MILDON, bestselling author of *The Soul Searcher's Handbook* and *Evolution of Goddess*

"This Pisces beauty is such an authentic go-to for healing, transformation, and deep soul nourishment. Like a siren, she calls you to your own inner depths, and I feel her messaging is an integral part of the healing of the feminine that is happening on the planet right now."

—NATALIA BENSON, women's empowerment coach and author of *Mystical AF*

"Alexandra is a powerhouse and this moving book reflects her story and others' stories. She shares with us for our own healing and growth potential. If you want to live fully alive, heal on a deep level, and step into the power that courses through you . . . read this book! Alexandra is unflinching in her storytelling! Her love for helping women heal from the deepest wounds of our crazy world is absolutely felt in her writing. What a voice! We need her NOW!"

—TONI BERGINS, founder of JourneyDance™, a Transformational Movement practice

F*CK LIKE A GODDESS.

HEAL YOURSELF.
RECLAIM YOUR VOICE.
STAND IN YOUR POWER.
F*CK LIKE A GODDESS.
ALEXANDRA ROXO

sounds true
BOULDER, COLORADO

Sounds True
Boulder, CO 80306

© 2020, 2023 Alexandra Roxo

Sounds True is a trademark of Sounds True, Inc.
All rights reserved. No part of this book may be used or reproduced in any
manner without written permission from the author(s) and publisher.

Published 2020, 2023

Book design by Nola Burger

Printed in the United States

BK06616

ISBN: 978-1-64963-052-0

The Library of Congress has cataloged the hardcover edition as follows:

Names: Roxo, Alexandra, author.
Title: F*ck like a goddess : heal yourself, reclaim your voice, stand in
   your power / by Alexandra Roxo.
Other titles: Fuck like a goddess
Description: Boulder, CO : Sounds True, 2020.
Identifiers: LCCN 2019036846 (print) | LCCN 2019036847 (ebook) | ISBN
   9781683643944 (hardback) | ISBN 9781683643951 (ebook)
Subjects: LCSH: Women--Psychology. | Self-actualization (Psychology) in
   women. | Femininity of God.
Classification: LCC HQ1155 .R69 2020 (print) | LCC HQ1155 (ebook) | DDC
   155.3/33--dc23
LC record available at https://lccn.loc.gov/2019036846
LC ebook record available at https://lccn.loc.gov/2019036847

10 9 8 7 6 5 4 3 2 1

FSC
www.fsc.org
MIX
Paper | Supporting
responsible forestry
FSC® C103098

THIS BOOK IS DEDICATED TO my mom and dad, to my teachers, and to all those hearts that have the courage to heal, to stand up, to question, to share, and to be beacons of change and love, paving the way for this awakening world.

CONTENTS

INTRODUCTION

CONGRATULATIONS. WELCOME. You made it. I know it probably wasn't easy to get here.

You may have grown up in a country where you were told that being you wasn't enough or perhaps that sex was bad, either directly or indirectly. Where you had to hide your sexuality or wildness or magical practices and keep them all behind closed doors, to be spoken about in whispers.

You may have been taught about a masculine version of the divine, a god, but not about a goddess or about the divine spark within you.

You may have grown up with a strict religion.

You may find the word "fuck" triggering.

You may find the word "god" triggering.

Whatever you are feeling in this moment is perfect, and...

I am so, so glad that you're here.

This means you are ready to experience a deeper layer of living and loving. Perhaps you are ready to be reunited with your sacred essence. Perhaps you are asking for more, because you know there is more to life than what you've been fed by the world. Perhaps you have shit you want to shake up.

We all have fears that keep us small. Traumas that we have endured, big and little, the imprints of which keep us afraid and stuck. Maybe you're sick of feeling anxious. Or of secretly hating your body. Perhaps you're feeling confused about what direction to take in life or how to share your voice with the world. Maybe you've sucked at romance. Or your experience of sex has been mainly not so great. Or your childhood wounds are annoyingly showing up in every relationship. I feel you. I know it's not easy.

The tough news is that we have each inherited a ton of stuff from our parents, not to mention the culture at large, and guess what—if we don't bring awareness to it, it ain't going nowhere! But the good news is that we each have the *innate* power to change those old patterns and, in doing so, to reclaim our bodies, the way that we love, our relationship to sex and to the divine, and so much more.

Sadly, it's not like we were given a how-to manual on how to get through it all (except that unspoken "Keep calm and carry on" contract you don't exactly remember signing). But trust me, you already have in you *all* the tools you need to have a rich, deep, magical life. They're inherent to your operating system. They're laced into your DNA. It's a matter of uncovering those hidden treasures using the arts that perhaps were not taught to you. The sacred arts of self-healing and of transformation. And this is what we are going to begin to do together.

Not that it will necessarily be easy or happen overnight. After all, uncovering your *full essence* is a radical act. It could take lifetimes. But why not begin to dive into the depths of your spirit now and transform anything inhibiting you from experiencing the depth of your love?

For transformation to occur, there must be a container, a substance to be transformed (a pattern, belief, fear, et cetera), and the energy or heat to make it happen. In this book I will lead you through the creation of your container, guide you to the awareness to see the patterns or fears dictating your life, and provide practices to help you create the energy for their transformation.

It is the act of taking your healing process into your own hands. It is standing up and saying:

I am willing to show up even when it's uncomfortable,
to claim the freedom to become all that I want to be.
To shine brightly even amid the dark.
To love as big as I possibly can.
To make love to life.
To the present moment.
To myself.
To a lover.
To the sky.
To let myself be the ever evolving who-I-am and let that
    discovery be my life's art.
To reclaim my body, my voice, my power,
And when it hurts
I will not give up!
Because I will be thinking of Mama Earth and how she
    needs me to shine
And I will be thinking of little boys and girls who are not free
And I will let my battle cry be:
I will find courage to face my fears.
I will love big even when it hurts.
I will not avoid the tough stuff, but take as many breaks
    as I need.
I will *open* to this life.
I will awaken.
For the sake of all beings everywhere.
And so it is.

Let this be your anthem. Or write your own. Read it aloud to yourself, under your breath. And any time you feel anxious or catch yourself going to say, "Nah, I'm good. Life is fine," or you spiral into self-hate or shame or guilt or fear, or you numb out with TV or wine, or you bury yourself in being busy and forget about your heart, come back to this anthem. Make it your manifesto of awakening. Your statement of loving intent. For the earth, your family, your parents, your babies . . .

But most of all . . . *for you.*

Because the world needs your wholeness now. And don't you want to feel a return to the infinite *you* in this life? A sweet reunion with your full, wild heart?

You are a vitally important piece of the ecosystem and well-being of this planet. Do not forget it. And when you heal yourself, reclaim your voice, stand in your power, and show up to the world more alive and vibrant and ecstatic as a result, you will inspire others to do the same. I've seen the ripple effect . . . in effect! And it is amazing. This is when you begin to wake other people the fuck up with your spirit. By simply being *you.*

The messy, wild, weird, nerdy, silly, deep, multifaceted, ever-changing *you.*

My wish is that you use this book as a manual for reclaiming anything and everything that you feel has been taken from you and that you commit to a spirit of magic and discovery, a life of deep and open living and loving.

That you use this to feel alive and in your body every day, to put down the heavy baggage you've inherited from your family, and to shine full-megawatt bright in the world, owning your wholeness and not dimming your light for anyone or anything.

Promise yourself that you won't give up and that you'll keep unraveling and unpeeling and deep diving into the gorgeous being that you are.

Every.

Mother.

Fucking.

Day.

My Story

Before we embark on this journey together, let me tell you why *I* am here. Why I care so much about love, healing, art, fucking, and awakening. And why I am so passionate about showing you that anything is possible and that there is a deeper level to living and loving that is accessible to us all.

I've overcome some things in my life. I've danced the good dance with my fears and woes, just like you. I've found magic in dark caverns of my being, turning wounds into allies, foes into friends.

My own karmic material in this life, which I have used as fuel for transformation, has included sexual traumas and the symptoms arising from those experiences; childhood imprinting due to separation from my parents; feelings of abandonment and of being unloved and unlovable, as well as the emotional patterns that emerged from those feelings, including anxiety, depression, disordered eating, and body dysmorphia; patterns of lack around money; codependency from growing up with traumatized and depressed parents... the list is seemingly endless. All this has been the material I have brought into my transformational work. I have graduated from these patterns and symptoms preventing me from loving, living, embodying truth, and I have reached a place where they do not dictate or shape my reality. Some of them I haven't seen in years.

Others echo here and there, yet I have changed my relationship to them, and I no longer fear them. This is the power of personal transformation. We have the capacity to change our deepest fears, patterns, and neuroses into sources of love and power.

Many people get lost in the deep, dark caverns of those experiences and symptoms. And I have done so at times, but ultimately I have chosen a life of doing the opposite. I have asked *all* the pains, traumas, and patterns to wake me up to exactly who I am today.

I think of it like the personal history degree (PhD) in Earth School chosen by my precise karmic makeup, creating the space for alchemy in my heart and soul, making me the exact walking, talking medicine I am now. And I would not trade any of it, as weird as that may sound.

I have also had 1,001 wild and fun adventures that have likewise woken me up and crafted me as life art from Earth School. I have experienced fun and laughter and big love. I have traveled the world. Swum naked in phosphorescent waters under a full moon. Meditated in caves in Nepal with Tibetan monks. Wrapped snakes around my body in a ceremony of ancient dance. Hitchhiked with truckers through the Southwest. Made documentaries in Cuba and New Mexico and Brazil.

There have been magazine interviews about my work and film premieres.

Dates with famous actors and dance parties into the night.

Sex where my body has turned into stars and I have been unable to speak for hours after, where I felt like I was on MDMA for five days straight, because the experience was so ecstatic.

People have written me poems, made me jewelry, sung me songs, and cried in my arms.

And I too have cried in the arms of many.

I've stood on stages in front of hundreds of women and watched them weep as I told my stories and they shared their fears with the room.

I've lived a good life, a *big* life. I am very blessed to have had the conditions and the courage to do so.

And it is all this life experience that's led me to where I am now. At the time of writing this, it has been four years since I expanded from being an award-winning filmmaker and having a career of artistic expression to working full-time in the healing arts and writing, to help women find their voices, heal themselves, and come back to wholeness.

The women I work with have experienced many difficulties, from sexual assaults to uncontrollable anxiety to being afraid of being seen and the gamut of other obstacles that many modern women face simply in attempting to live a conscious, meaningful life. It has been my pleasure to lead other women in the art of healing and transformation, supporting them to step outside of the status quo and live from an open heart.

My work in this field started with a voice within that told me it was time to change *my* life and finally face some of my own wounding in a deeper way than I had. It was a voice I heard in an ayahuasca ceremony. Perhaps you've heard of this amazing, albeit somewhat terrifying, plant medicine. I like to call her one of my main teachers. She told me to wake the fuck up, stop caring about being famous, about being ambitious, about how I looked, and instead to go out and help people before I self-destructed. I did *exactly* as she said. And, funnily enough, it's been smooth sailing since then (relatively speaking), and many things have fallen into place as I heeded the call to dive deeper into my soul's calling and my own transformational journey.

Since that day, I have worked with hundreds of women around the world, supporting, mentoring, and leading them toward having the courage to come back to themselves and share their stories with the world.

The seeds of this path were there in my early career as an artist and filmmaker, when I set out, at the age of eighteen, to study life. But what I really wanted to discover was what it means to be a woman. I was curious about why women's stories had been left out of most of the spiritual texts across the globe. Why no one was talking about how many women experienced sexual assaults. Why women were expected to diet and starve themselves or to change their appearance in other ways to be accepted. I was *very* confused about how this was all okay! Not to mention I was pissed. So I set out to make art that questioned *why* and *how* we got this way.

It was a path that led me to travel to Cuba and meet Fidel Castro's family. That found me filming dead bodies in morgues. There was the time I went undercover in brothels in New York City and worked with women who'd been victims of sex trafficking. There was the project where I traveled to a truck-stop strip club in New Mexico and lived and worked with the dancers there. Where I danced for men in my Converse sneakers and cotton undies and shot machine guns in the desert. Another where I spent two weeks living with girls on the streets interviewing them about their choices to live their lives on the fringe.

As I moved through these worlds, naïve and wise at the same time, I learned that underneath, as women, we are very similar. We all hurt. We all love. And we all have been through a lot of shit! Rich and poor, brown and white, straight and queer. Not to say we are the same or to downplay one culture's experiences of oppression or trauma, but indeed there is a thread that connects us.

I saw that many of us have been told our sexuality (however we identify) is too much for the world, that we need to be pretty in order to be lovable, and a whole slew of other things that seem designed to keep us separated from who we truly are. And I also saw that the act of sitting together and sharing stories was a way that we healed once before and that we needed to get back to. That when we cried together, ate together, sang together, and danced together, like the ancient people did, it worked.

What I found is that we already know the path back home to ourselves; there is no need to reinvent the wheel. Humans have been healing themselves for thousands of years. It's simply a wisdom that had been taken and squashed but is ripe for reclaiming,

We are all seeking the same thing: to feel like it's okay just to be *us*. We all have issues passed down to us, but most of the time, we don't know how and where to begin to grapple with them. And since the process also seems scary as fuck, it is easier to keep on saying: "I'm fine." And to just keep going. The people pleasing. The body hatred. The money fears. The not wanting to outshine others. A codependent need to "help others." The list goes on … and it's the matching baggage we are all carrying around. Showing up to dinner parties with three carry-ons. Going on first dates with a duffle bag of issues that would be marked heavy at airport check-in.

And so I have devoted myself to helping others like you, like *me*, with the unpacking and breaking-free process. And along the way, I have sought out many spiritual traditions, looking for refuge and spaces to do my own healing.

My spiritual path began with the Presbyterian Sunday school my mother sent me to from ages six to fifteen because she thought it would be good for me as an only child to be with other kids. Which it was, in some ways, but she must not have gotten the memo that no feelings are allowed in the Presbyterian church. Though I'm sure being cast as a "Sin City Dancer" from the bad city of Babylon in the church play when I was eight and wearing a red feather boa shaped my sexuality in ways I'll always be grateful for!

Then there was my Catholic grandma in Brazil, who would pray the rosary over me when I was sick with diarrhea. She kept giving me Brazilian tap water and wondering why I was doubled over in pain, and I remember her and five other old ladies thumbing plastic beads, praying over me while I lay in the middle of the floor like a sacrificial gringa lamb with knotted intestines, Vatican programming blaring from the TV.

I was introduced to neohippie spirituality when, at eighteen, I went to a Rainbow Gathering with my best friend, Rebecca, and we accidentally camped by the medical tent. We were kept up all night by a guy on a bad trip shouting, "I have the biggest motherfucking dick!" We also had to poop in a communal trough next to other people pooping, which meant I did not poop for approximately seven whole days due to terror of public pooping. I still somehow managed to dance around a drum circle, where I picked up a guy whom I later visited in Philly. When, on our date, he sang Bob Marley songs while busking on the side of the street with his guitar and hemp necklace and encouraged me to dance along, I was slightly mortified we were singing for our supper. If only I had known I would still be drawn to this archetype of human, the wandering visionary mystical artist, even almost twenty years later, I would have probably relaxed and enjoyed that moment more.

I found my way to Free Activist Witch Camp, where I slept under a blue plastic tarp in the Oregon woods and talked to fairies. I then studied Norse shamanism, Peruvian shamanism, Mexican shamanism, indigenous North American medicine, yoga, Kashmiri Shaivist tantra, tantric Buddhism, and neopaganism. I feel like my soul has been catching up on the teachings of the past lives I imagine I have lived all around the globe.

It is moon rituals and meditating and plant medicine work that have been the basis of my spiritual practice during the last period of my life, and they have been a lifeline. So much so that I created Moon Club (with my friend, the author Ruby Warrington), an online mentorship and coaching program where for three years I taught and shared and held space for thousands of other women who may live in towns and cities without access to such content in person.

I have healed and learned so much from all these years of study and exploration. However, one of my early observations has been proven time and again: most of these traditions and spaces have been run by men. What's more, behind the scenes, many spiritual leaders have assaulted and abused women and children. From Christianity to Tibetan Buddhism to swamis in the yoga world, stories of sexual abuse are rampant among spiritual men of power. So the question remains: as a woman, to whom do you turn for a deep, safe spiritual practice of healing and connection with the divine?

I turned within, and I learned to heal myself. I used my voice and my art. I used my body, and I asked for nature's help. And all of my work has led me to believe that it is time for us to step outside of the patriarchal model of spirituality and into a new era.

It is time for women, and anyone who doesn't identify as a cisgendered man, to become our own leaders and decision-makers and spiritual teachers—for ourselves and for one another. For an earth that is deeply hurting. Think of the thousands of women and children sold into sex trafficking and being raped, abused, and molested daily. Yes, it hurts my heart too. But I also want to be real. Real about 29.2 million acres a year of rain forest being lost to capitalist gains. Real about the fact that every five minutes one animal species is going extinct. I recently watched a documentary on Netflix that showed the last cheetahs and snow leopards, and I thought: "Damn, Apple. How dare you name a computer operating system Snow Leopard when David Attenborough just told me there are only fifty left?!" Similar feelings arise for Amazon, a multi-billion-dollar business named after our Earth's largest rainforest, which is under major ecological threat. This is our world. It's wild and wacky and weird and so, so sad at times. And yet, I am *not* giving up on it.

I believe the pain so many of us feel on a personal level is a reflection of the pain that is so rife on our planet—and that it is going to take a reimagining of all structures, including the ways in which we worship and heal, in order to make the changes we need. And hey, it may take lifetimes, but I am willing to do the work *now* so the children coming after me experience a healthier world. And maybe don't have to deal with some of the shit we did.

Which means I want you to commit to fucking life, to making love to it, becoming one with it like the goddess/divine being you are, for your own happiness and well-being... and also for *us*.

I want to show you *how*, through my journey and what I have experienced with people I have worked with. How I overcame the traumas and the pain. How I learned to love my body. How I found relationships that celebrate and nurture me. How I got the courage to shine brightly in the world. How I found my unique voice. And how I created a life for myself in which I get to do what I love and make good money doing it.

Thank you again for being on this journey with me. Now, let me remind you that anything is possible and that you too can live and love the life you already have.

How to Use This Book

The main chapters of this book are designed to walk you through the process of reclaiming, opening, awakening, and healing that I have used on myself and with my clients to stand up, to shine, to speak up, and to live as an embodied, awakened being.

You can read this book from start to finish. Or you can flip to a ritual or a practice that is calling you and skip directly to that. At the end of each step to becoming the fully embodied, magical being that you are, I will provide a few simple ways to practice putting the teachings and ideas and values I am sharing into motion in your life, so change can happen fluidly and fast.

Set a timeline to do this work, if that feels like it would help, and aim to spend one to two weeks with each section. If you are a person who functions well with support and community, you can find groups to work with through my website (alexandraroxo.com/flag). You'll also find all the accompanying practices, guided meditations, and bonus materials I mention there.

Like I said, the exercises in this book reflect the *exact* processes and practices I lead myself and my clients through. Over the years, I have spent thousands of hours with myself and with women just like you, working on unblocking our hearts and bodies and guiding us into a deeper level of presence, radiance, and connection to ourselves—into our wholeness. The protocols I share in this book have led to countless breakthroughs. I have witnessed many women's victories as they plowed through the toughest shit and into their radiance! And more than anything I have witnessed my own victories.

This is usually really private and personal work, though it can also be done with a friend so that you can hold each other safely as you open these vaults and closets. There is nothing to show or to prove. The goal is simply to accept your experiences, to integrate them, and in doing so to reclaim the energy it was taking to keep them hidden in the shadows, freeing you to live as your full-power you.

If you are doing it with a friend, you may notice that when a particularly triggering chapter comes up, suddenly you guys both get really busy or one of you just isn't into the book anymore. Well, this is when you dive in even deeper and *keep going*. In fact, however you approach this work, some resistance will likely come up, tricking you into saying things like "Fuck this! I'm fine! I don't need healing!" Our minds are *smart* like that. My mind has tricked me into thinking all kinds of things as it tries to protect me from the unknown territory of my next massive expansion.

It's up to you to pace yourself and to commit. To remember to breathe deeply. And also to say, "Hi, mind. I am safe. I am not going to fall apart. I am choosing to grow. I am *ready* to grow. I know you just want me to be safe, but I'm good. I can handle this."

When the resistance comes, it may also feel like being tired, foggy, angry, or grumpy. We all have our resistance flavors, the ways that we prevent ourselves from moving closer to the edge of expansion. Because the truth is we have *zero* clue what's beyond that edge. We may fall off into oblivion, for all we know! And so the mind tries to convince us to stay put. It's doing its job to make sure we survive. Bless its heart! But while some of the work we do together might feel scary, none of it is dangerous. If anything, the aim is to remind you that you're so powerful, you have no need to fear anything!

At the end of each chapter there will be transformational work, exercises, rituals, and practices that are *key* to making shifts and will become the core of your work. This is you becoming your own coach or healer and starting to move energy for yourself, to work your shit out, and to *transform* yourself. Yes, you can self-heal. In fact, it is your birthright.

So don't skip these parts. Think of how strong and badass and courageous and yummy you'll feel afterward. You may feel like, "Nah, I already know this. I'm good. I'll skip ahead!" (Remember what I said about resistance.) But I urge you to take it slow. To spend time with the work. And to have fun with it wherever you can.

It's up to you to claim the space to expand. As Anaïs Nin, one of my favorite writers since I was a teen, wrote: "And the day came when the risk to remain tight in a bud was more painful than the risk it took to blossom." You will know when it's actually become more uncomfortable to *not* grow. In fact, I am guessing that is why you are here.

My promise to you is that if you do the work, you will see and feel palpable results. But it takes commitment. It takes practice. There may be tears. Okay, likely there *will* be tears. And it is all 100 percent necessary.

Because there will also likely be bursts of ecstatic *joy*. There will be sexy-as-hell moments and waves of bliss as you come home to more and more of your heart and soul. Trust me on this one.

Buckle Your Safety Belt: A Few Disclaimers

On Mental Health

Anytime we do work on ourselves, it is up to us to be responsible and real about where we are at. You are responsible for your own safety here, and while resistance is one thing, if you need to take a breather, have a cry, do some yoga, shake it out, or call a friend, *please do.* Sometimes, depending on what we have been through, we get triggered—old parts of us that are hard to handle get activated or brought to the surface. Simply *talking* about sex is uncomfortable for many people! That is okay. It's not a sign to abandon ship—it's a sign that you are moving some old stuff and getting closer to an expansion. But sometimes it can be overwhelming. So breathe, relax, and take your time.

If you have mental health struggles, make sure you also tell your therapist or coach that you are going to be opening some dusty old closets. Let your partner, a parent, or a friend know, too. And I am trusting you to know when something is too much for you. If you ever feel like you're veering into too dark a cavern, ask for help, call a friend or a hotline. There is zero to be ashamed of. I have sent text messages in the past saying, "Um, hi. I'm having some dark thoughts. I just wanted to let a friend know."

On Gender

This book can be used by anyone of any age and of *any* gender identity or expression. I will talk about my journey as a cisgendered woman, as this is the only life experience I have. I have a menstrual cycle and a pussy/yoni/cervix/vulva in my physical body, and this may not apply to all, and that is okay. Take what works and leave the rest. *Everyone*, of every gender expression, can develop their relationship to the divine feminine, masculine, or nongendered imagining of the divine. Everyone can heal and fuck like a goddess/ wild one/love being or whatever element of divinity you choose to embody. So if the pronouns I use don't work for you, please substitute what does and make this book your own.

On Lineage

And lastly, I want to honor all cultures, all peoples, and all traditions that I have worked with personally and that I mention in this book. Modern conversations about spirituality can often be an eclectic melting pot of ideas, practices, songs, and myths without roots. As you now know, I have been a deep seeker of spiritual knowledge my whole life, and I consider myself an always and forever student in this realm. As such, I acknowledge that my personal path has been influenced by many cultures and traditions from around the world. Whatever I am passing on to you, know that it is part of my own practice to do so with 100 percent integrity. My intention in sharing everything you find in this book is to help you, to guide you, and to remind you of your true and most profound, innate divine nature.

And a Note about Privilege

I also acknowledge that as a white woman, I am speaking and teaching from a very specific point of view, which is the card I have been dealt in this life. This means some of my personal experiences may not resonate with everybody who reads this book.

Many women have suffered a thousand times more than I truly understand. Part of the work I've done with clients, in my articles, and in my feature films and documentaries has been to highlight stories of women of all ethnicities, cultures, and backgrounds, since the mainstream media is often a one-sided, brainwashed, and whitewashed space. But this book is told from my perspective, as it is based on a deeply personal journey.

In sharing my stories as honestly and with as much integrity as I can, my hope is to show that there are *parts* of us and of our lived experience that transcend race, gender, and sexual preference. That connecting with each other from this place is part of how we heal and become whole.

WHAT IT MEANS TO FUCK LIKE A GODDESS

BEFORE I REMIND YOU how to heal yourself, reclaim your voice, and stand in your power, let's talk about the title of this book. The word "fuck" comes from a fourteenth-century Dutch and Swedish word, and at its root it means "to breed." I am using it here mainly because it packs a punch. Here are some of my favorite "fuck" expressions:

"Fuck it!"
Meaning, "Let it go!"

"I wanna fuck."
Meaning, "I wanna make raw and passionate love!"

"I don't fuck with that."
Meaning, "I don't engage with that."

Those are my interpretations, of course, but I *love* this word. The fact it can be used in any situation where we want to make an *impact* speaks to the inherent power of the act it was originally used to describe: i.e., the act of *creation*! This power can make you squirm in your seat, very much like *your* own innate wild and mysterious power, and that is why I'm using it here.

Whoever taught us that making love or fucking was solely about physical intercourse missed the point. To me, it's to come into a divine union with. A divine communion with. Whether you are physically or metaphorically "fucking," it can mean taking in the energy of creation so deeply that you feel you are making love to your life and that divine creation energy is moving through you. That you are becoming one with the source of all that is. I mean, why do we say, "I'm cumming" when we orgasm? It's like, "Damn! I'm finally arriving! I'm showing up to the wholeness of who I am! I am embodying this infinite, ecstatic, wild, messy, creative force that I was born to be."

As for the "Goddess" part, this word represents the feminine version of God. "She" has been cut out of much of Western history and religion, and I feel *very* passionate about bringing her back. And yet we can experience the divine in nongendered ways, as a creative spark inside of each of us, which is important and great—and it's also important to examine *why* the notion of the Goddess, or the divine feminine, has been subjugated by the dominant paradigms of the patriarchy throughout history.

If you grew up in the Western world, chances are you grew up with an idea of "God" as a grumpy old white man hanging out in the clouds. Perhaps you got exposed to something a little more progressive than that, and this "God" was loving and fatherly... as well as super strict. But chances are that, unless you are a part of a small population living outside of regular society, you grew up with a male "God" figure or male religious leaders and the female figures in whatever religion you were exposed to were simply not as important. The teachers were mainly men.

On a day-to-day level, this has also manifested as many qualities identified as feminine (a sense of nurturing, a mama-bear type of protectiveness, a fierceness that doesn't allow people and the earth to be hurt, a softness in the heart, a sexual radiance, a capacity to feel, to name a few) being considered "too much" or weak or else not being accepted in the workplace or other patriarchal capitalist environments. The patriarchal way of doing things doesn't leave much space for feelings, be it sadness, rage, or ecstasy. The structures that govern our lives are built on hierarchy—and instead of the emphasis being on our collective growth, these structures thrive off power, privilege, and wealth, which are disseminated (or not) from the top down.

Now, if you grew up in a non-Western space or a noncapitalist or nonpatriarchal environment, you may have been shown a female version of divinity. Something that you could relate to and be mirrored by, thus helping you to remember that you yourself are an expression of this face of the divine, too. And perhaps you experienced alternative structures within which you learned, shared, grieved, created, and grew. Believe it or not, there are places in the world where these models are thriving!

Everyone's experience of religion, spirituality, divinity will be different, and that is okay.

But those of us who grew up with a masculine depiction of the divine and who are not cisgendered men have been sent messages of unworthiness or of being less than. Sometimes subtly: "Hmm, so weird there are only a few women mentioned in the Bible, must be a mistake!" wondered the eight-year-old me. And sometimes more directly: "Wow! Women exist in the Bible as virgin, whore, and mother! Which one am I?!" wondered fifteen-year-old me, looking in the mirror at her leopard-print Victoria's Secret G-string while listening to Outkast. Did not resonate with virgin or mother. You get the gist.

These messages have been embedded into our subconscious to the point that we don't even realize they're there. It has been communicated to us, often silently, that the female body is sinful, or messy, or dirty, or simply lesser. We've been told that our bodies need to be hidden away or "protected" from the desires of men.

Society has also taught us, women and feminine beings and any other beings who may be perceived as "other" by the patriarchal power structures, that we are the ones who get fucked. That we can't really *do* the fucking, in sex and in life. And this idea has left its imprint on the way we walk through the world, the way we embody the divine, the way we make love to it all.

But the massive truth is that the energy of nature, of Mother Earth, of Creation itself, is also the most powerful energy in the cosmos—so powerful that thousands of years of patriarchy has tried to push it down, squeeze it into corsets, put it up onto wobbly heels, burn it at the stake, and lock it behind closed doors. In the most extreme examples of the suppression and eradication of the Goddess and the wisdom of the earth, this energy has been persecuted with witch hunts and trials and the genocides of indigenous peoples. And all of this has been happening *for a very long time.*

But times have changed! Thanks to the efforts of many strong and fierce women and othered peoples, over the past century, the full-spectrum divine is emerging once again to reclaim its place in this physical realm. Women (and men and nonbinary folks alike) are realizing we are now free to use the energy of creation, or *sex*, which moves through all of us, to create and live lives we truly love, in contrast to how this energy was used and abused prior. Yes, we still have a ways to go. And that's why it is essential, first and foremost, that we do the work on ourselves to wake up and show up.

And while I want to teach you how to fuck like a "goddess," a large part of our work together here exists outside of typical spiritual or religious or societal norms or programming about divinity.

It is bringing spirit into matter. It's not woo-woo. It's blood, sweat, and tears. And it can feel like magic.

The turn-of-the-century occultist Dion Fortune defined magic as "the art of changing consciousness at will," which I learned from the seminal teacher and pioneer Starhawk. In my work, this translates as: the art of changing old energy that we have inherited from our families or that has stuck around from pain or trauma into something new. This regenerative process is at the heart of our healing, and it certainly feels magical. It's like the way cow poop gets used as fertilizer for seeds to grow in and become beautiful flowers. If turning shit to roses isn't magical, I don't know what is!

Inviting the Divine Back into Your Physical Being: From Worship to Embodiment

If you have a womb, a clit, and a cervix in your physical body, then:

- You have a *physical* portal where creation enters.

- It is available not just for baby making.

- It is available for you to access sexual and creative energy and let it radiate through your actions, words, and vibes—without it being linked to a sexual experience.

- It is available for you to experience healing through mind-blowing orgasms.

- It is up to you to own and reclaim those parts from the negative conditioning that religion, society, culture, or even your family has imprinted.

And if you do not have the physical attributes stated above, as a conscious human being you are still perfectly equipped to channel and embody this creative energy. You just have a different physical operating system for connecting to it that I have personally not lived in. All good. You can create your own energetic womb, like a sacred inner altar, for embodying and channeling these vibes whenever you want.

Allowing yourself to get to know those parts more deeply, without guilt or shame or fear, is important. Massively healing. Allowing them to be sacred, magical, buzzing with energy is also a source of power that I want you to experience. And that you are 100 percent able to do.

Claiming and accepting your *own* divinity—the fact that you are a direct reflection of source—is it. It is when you get to walk down the street feeling synched with life. Feeling like you belong. Because now you are a moving, walking, talking part of nature *herself,* an integral piece of the magical mystery of the divine. And when you try and hide her...well, you're battling with a force far stronger than you. This is when she will call you home to her, with period cramps, with gut intuition that says, "Do not go out with him!" You'd better believe, she will never stop whispering into your ears—despite the skinny jeans, the hard-core workouts, the busy schedules, the double lattes, and whatever else the fuck we think we have to have in order to keep it together in this modern world.

In fact, it's when we cut this inner energy *off* that shit gets weird. When we dim our own power, whether in abusive relationships, or by going along with the exclusionary or oppressive messages of popular culture, or by simply not speaking up, this is when we get sick. Our periods stop. We get irritable bowel syndrome (IBS). We learn to hate our bodies. And in this shutting down, we also close down our connection to the divine. We close ourselves to the power running through us.

How does the divine, magical sparkle of creation speak to us?

In tears that well up and drip down your face when you see another human suffering.

In thunderstorms that come out of nowhere.

In orgasms that make you laugh, and then cry, and then feel a peace like you've never known.

When your period comes on the exact day you have to take time off.

In the million other heart tugs and belly butterflies and inner knowings that are coming to us all the time.

Begin to listen carefully, and you will know when you hear her. And when you have lost the connection, there are so many ways to tune back in:

You can swim naked in the sea.

You can dance wildly in your underwear.

You can share a true story that hurts your heart with a dear friend.

You can stop and get quiet.

You can write your heart out in the pages of your journal.

I am going to share with you so many ways in the pages of this book, so you never have to worry again about what GPS system to use to find your way home to that glorious heart in you.

Sexual Healing

As we begin to investigate the collective sexual shadow and do our own sexual healing, we also begin to reframe our sexual experiences as another *brilliant* portal to divine magic.

A major piece that I find missing from a lot of wellness and spiritual spaces is talk about real sex—sexuality, desire, the pain of sexual abuse, and inherited sexual trauma. Looking at this stuff can be scary as fuck, so we often just leave it out. But this is leaving out the *essence* of us. We keep sex hidden in therapists' rooms, in bedrooms with lights out, under covers and blankets, and behind locked doors. *Why?* Because of the heaps of shame about sex that we are suffocating under. That you and me, right now, are overturning! The conditioning we have received about sex is crusty and stale, and slowly we are culturally moving away from it. But try mentioning a sexual story at a dinner party with your close friends or in a healing circle. Or imagine what would happen if you responded to "What's been up with you?" with "I just had a mind-blowing orgasm where I saw my grandmothers gathered around me in a blessing!" The point being, it often feels like our sexual stories are still *too much*, even for spaces and people we trust. They feel too weird, too risky, too intense, too triggering, and so we keep them in, and all that untapped power stays locked within us. And the dominant paradigm keeps being able to use sex to control us, packaging it and selling it in ways that don't look or feel authentic to most of us. We must speak up, claim ourselves, and create the changes we are thirsty for.

Ultimately, fucking like a god/goddess/wise one/firecracker/love light or whatever you identify with means honoring the divine spark in *you*—which means a shift *away* from lives constructed around capitalist ideas about success, business, or family. It means honoring a *flow* that is bigger than you, a flow that is like nature. One minute it's sunny. The next, the clouds have rolled in. A breeze picks up. Then a lightning bolt cracks. Thunder rolls, and a rain shower falls. And only thirty minutes later, there's a rainbow in the sky.

This is how the divine flow of wild creation energy rolls. Like a wild, primal force you cannot control. And when you try to control it or suppress it, it will rebel. (Which is where we find ourselves on the whole as a human race at this moment.)

Your orgasms will become strained. The light in your eyes will dwindle. You'll find yourself putting on more shine powder. More eyeliner. More perfume. Trying to revive the natural beauty that seems to have dulled. You'll look for inner light in gold jewelry and diamond rings. In bigger breasts that scream, "I am one with nature! Look, nature, Goddess is moving through me and I am *fecund*, ripe with life! Just see! My tits reflect that!" (That's been me pushing my A cups into Victoria Secret's "Bombshell bras" since I was thirteen and then sneaking them off in public because I feel like a phony and the wire is poking me.) And all of this is *fine*, by the way. It's how we've learned to look for nature and the divine in a world that has kept it hidden and smushed down. What I have found after searching in tubes of Russian Red MAC lipstick, in barre classes, in self-help books, and in just about every spiritual tradition, is that true *light*, the true *fuck*, the wild mystery, comes from within. And that it's actually easier to reach than we think.

When a woman lets that power free to run through her like a wildfire, she is unstoppable. Look at Beyoncé. To me, she is the embodiment of raw sex and power and freedom! She lets the *divine flow* move through her body. Her voice. Her eyes. Her laugh. She is at once insanely powerful and scary, devastating as a tsunami, *and* as soft as gentle rain.

Trying to create an agenda for how and when the divine guides us won't work. You cannot schedule a rainstorm. You cannot book a meeting with a rainbow. You just let it come. You surrender, you move out of the way, you create the conditions for an opening to occur. And then you let go.

As for how we do *that?* Well, that's what I'm going to begin to share with you in this book, in depth, from my heart and soul and body, as best as I know how.

How to Make Space for Magic to Happen In

In order to transform, to heal, to make magic, to expand, you need a container. A "container" is a word for a safe and intentional space for you to do your healing, crafting, becoming, and transforming, literally and energetically. You might look at this as your magical chamber of alchemy. A literal altar. An internal space for change to occur in. Space for your magic.

Why do we need this? Energy needs to be contained, or it disperses. When you open a bottle of water and you want to make tea with it, you need another container, a tea kettle, to transform it into tea. You don't just pour it on the floor and hope the tea will happen! The water needs to be contained, in a very specific way, with some *heat* thrown in, so it can boil. In the same way, your power, your voice, your *magic* needs a container, so it doesn't just leak all over the place and evaporate.

This means you will need three things to do our work, aka magical crafting, together: a safe physical space; space in your emotional life; and a little space in your calendar. With this as your foundation, the rest can flow as you go.

There is a difference between creating rigid structures and simply creating strong containers. A container could look like the space created between you and two besties getting together each month on the full moon to talk about where you're at, share a meditation, have dinner, and write down some things you're working on. Getting too rigid about it would be allotting fifteen minutes in your daily schedule and expecting the magic to show up on demand, enabling a transformation in the time between your breakfast and your morning commute. Can you feel the difference?

Over time your containers will become stronger, meaning the divine will get the memo that you are serious about all this, and energy will flow more freely there. It's the difference between meeting fifteen friends once a month for a brief coffee date versus sharing weekly meetings with three of your closest friends, spending more time together, and allowing for trust, deep insights, and intimacy to occur.

Feel into the difference in the containers of those friendships. As you see those three friends weekly, the container of your friendship gets stronger and stronger, and therefore it can hold much more. It can hold fights, meltdowns, ideas, business jams, and chats about the crazy, intense, *real* shit. And that is the work we'll be doing together here.

Some Spaces to Make Magic In

I have also come to know what containers work for me over time, through practice and trial and error. When I begin work with my clients, before I even say yes to working with them, I make sure they have three core things in place or are willing to get them solid before we begin. They need to have community, meaning support in terms of family or a few good friends. They need some sort of a daily practice, so they can have a space for grieving, singing, and envisioning whatever we are working on. And they need to have the basics of self-care down: eating and sleeping well, engaging in some physical movement. If these core things are not in place, then we are attempting to rebuild and rearrange a house without a solid foundation, and it could crumble! We want to have that solid foundation before we start doing any major work. It doesn't mean those things are perfect. Some days you won't eat well or meditate, and that's life, but knowing how to get back to a state of balance is key.

Here's how to create some containers in your life. The first three have been essential for me, and from there you can see what else resonates with you.

Daily Practice

Whether engaging in healing work, trying to quiet anxiety, or becoming more productive, having a daily practice is an essential container for your personal growth, for spiritual maintenance, and for welcoming your wholeness home, again and again.

Establishing a daily practice can mean a lot of different things, and it can and will shift as you grow and change. When I was nineteen, it was twenty minutes of seated one-point-focus meditation and three pages in my journal (a practice I got from Julia Cameron's seminal book *The Artist's Way*). I have been cultivating this container ever since, and sometimes I take a break. But I still always write my morning pages—as a place for the divine flow to speak to me, for creative ideas to arrive, for feelings to be felt, and for dreams to be dreamed.

When it comes to meditation, there are so many different kinds, some more mind-oriented, some more heart-oriented, and some more body-oriented. I've included some recorded meditations and practices on alexandraroxo.com/flag for you to try. I highly recommend committing to *one* for at least forty days so you can go deep with it.

You may also paint every morning.

You may dance.

You may cry.

You may sing.

You may eye gaze with yourself in the mirror.

You may play guitar.

You may do kundalini yoga.

Any and all of this is *brilliant*—and doing it *every day* will create a deep container so that *divine fuck* energy can begin to find you.

For me: breath work is *essential*, meditation is essential, dance is essential, writing is essential, and singing! It sounds like a lot, but it keeps me in my peace and courage, keeps me lit, keeps me flowing and alive!

Our nervous systems are holding more than ever these days, with the computer and Internet and the busy-busy living that we are doing. If we don't work to expand and strengthen the nervous system, then anxiety levels will *rise*, and we won't be able to blast off into our lives. Daily practice is *so, so, so* essential to shining bright and standing in your power. *Trust me.*

Friendship + Community

As I mentioned above, cultivating deep community and friendships and gathering together are key to your expansion. In Buddhism this community may be called a *sangha*. In Hinduism and yogic traditions this spiritual gathering can be called a *satsang*. I don't know what we call in the West, to be honest, but we need it, and I think we've lost touch with how much we need it.

Why do we need like-minded and like-hearted humans around? Because they become our divine mirrors. They show us what we ourselves cannot see. They reflect our flaws ... *and* our magic. They hold us accountable. They help us with the lessons we need to learn in order to rise out of the past, and they become vehicles for our growth. This requires trust. You can't ask just anyone to be your divine mirror! Again, a deep container of community is something to develop over time. And having this is so, *so* powerful.

This could mean you gather with one or two trusted and close friends, but make it super regular and intentional. Or it could be that you bring together a group of women to meet every new or full moon. It could be a church group. A yoga group. Or simply a group of women all working on self-acceptance. However you go about creating your circle, meet at least monthly to share practices and go deep. This is how people across the globe for millennia have celebrated spiritual practice, nature, rites of passage, transitions, and the like. In the age of social media and smartphones, gathering intentionally off-line, heart to heart and face to face, is even *more* important to prioritize. If you feel stuck there, try Meetup, a local meditation center, a *kirtan* circle, a yoga class, or somewhere else where you can begin to meet other people on the path.

For the deep magic to occur in person, this is a space where I recommend refraining from drinking, or gossiping, or chitchatting. You can mix and mingle afterward if you want, but keep the container strong with some sort of structure and intentionality. For example, perhaps each person gets ten minutes to share. Or someone leads a meditation, or reads a poem, or brings a piece of writing to read. Having an agreed-upon structure for the gathering creates room for depth.

If you don't already have a few good people you trust to share space with in this way, then I want you to make finding them your mission. Because we cannot heal alone. We cannot transform alone. We cannot stand as the amazing humans we are alone. It just doesn't work that way. As we begin this work, find a group or circle or create your own.

Well-Being

When you want to grow, transform, expand, and become more *you*, it's essential to look after your physical body. This doesn't mean you have to be 100 percent "well" or "cured" (what does that even mean?!) of whatever is going on with you. It simply means that unless you are sleeping well, eating well, moving your body, and *including* your body in your greater healing process, you can't open more deeply and feel fully alive and thriving.

We all go through phases when life gets busy and our well-being gets put on the back burner, but our body itself is a vital container to keep *solid* as we grow. Prioritizing your well-being will help you feel your feelings in real time and literally *heal your shit* as you step into full power. This means getting to know your body. For example, I was a vegetarian off and on for fifteen years before I discovered I was protein, vitamin D, and iron deficient, and I have since made adjustments to replenish my resources. Who knows how many years I had been operating at less than full power and tolerating pain and discomfort? I've watched many women around me battle health issues in order to become strong enough to speak up, to share, to shine. If we are looking to grow and expand and are not taking into account the amount of sugar we eat, or the little sleep we are getting, or the five cups of coffee a day we are drinking, then we can only get so far.

In order to fully show up to life, we must fully show up to ourselves first. Because we have only one body. And we must care for it! I know if I show up to a party tired, hungry, and thirsty, I will be less present. I will be distracted and way less able to connect with the flow inside of me! I'll be scanning the room for the hors d'oeuvres. I'll be checking my phone because I'm too tired to talk.

You may know all this stuff, but it is *so* important to add check-ups into your routine. Take a blood test for vitamin levels, thyroid tests, even tests for your bowels if you have had IBS or potentially have leaky gut or food allergies. This is essential. Trust me, I had bad IBS my whole life, and until I sat down with a doctor and examined the results of my stool test, I had *zero* idea what was going on in my gut. Together, she and I fixed leaky gut, cleared candida, and even killed two kinds of parasites! (All that Brazilian tap water I drank as a kid while visiting Grandma?!)

The same thing goes for charting and understanding your menstrual cycle if you bleed. It is essential to know where your hormones are at and how they are affecting what's going on in your body. I also had irregular periods for years, which I believe was because I was living in a super-coffee-fueled, fast-paced kind of way as I zipped around New York City with jam-packed days, tight pants, and music blasting in my ears. Nature wants us to *slow down* when we bleed, so she can speak to us, so we can shed and regenerate. But I didn't have time for that! I kept up with the high-intensity classes, double lattes, and skinny jeans, trying to hold everything in tight... until a visit to a Chinese doctor whipped me into shape, and I changed my lifestyle completely. She made me throw out my pencil skirts and stop with the iced drinks ASAP! That plus herbs and some more changes, and my period returned, my cramps lessened, and my anxiety levels dropped in big ways. For more on this I highly recommend the work of Alisa Vitti, her book *WomanCode*, and her menstrual tracking app.

Sacred Space

When beginning your practice of self-healing/power-claiming/magic-making and radical expanding, having a dedicated sacred space to do it in becomes *key*! This can be a corner of your room or desk with a few sacred items, or it can be a whole room, a tiny cottage, an attic, or a place in your garden. It can be as elaborate as having sheepskin rugs and meditation cushions and crystals and framed pictures of people who inspire you, or it can be one simple candle, a stone, and a card from your favorite deck. For many years I have had tiny altars in many rooms, draped with colorful cloths from thrift stores or decorated with bouquets of flowers, sometimes with pieces of art, and I let these be my "inspiration corners" of sorts, where I do my most magical works, grieving, crafting, and envisioning. My sacred spaces are very special to me; whether small and portable or elaborate, they anchor me.

You can also create a sacred space in a closet away from the kids or in a cabinet that opens. Be creative! The physical space anchors your work in your reality.

Nature

The natural world is a perfect container for our growth, metaphorically and quite literally. From the cycles of the moon and how they impact us as beings to the million reflections of metamorphosis in nature, the natural world offers a beautiful symbolic mirror of our growth. There is space, there is flow, and there is chaos. There is truly everything you need to be reminded you are a part of a greater whole.

As you are experiencing the discomfort that comes with changing and evolving, look to nature to remind you, "Hey, you! This is normal! Just check out the trees shedding their leaves. Maybe that feels uncomfortable for the tree, too!" This connection and correlation feels really fucking good when you're going through a growth spurt and the growing pains *suck*.

You may have outgrown your job or friends. You may have had a spiritual epiphany and feel like you don't belong anywhere. You may feel confused about what's next. This is when you find a spot to be with nature. A tree you like to sit with in the park. A flower you water. A place you go to in the woods. In many Western cultures, we are not taught to interact with nature. Nature has often been seen as a commodity to be bought and sold, something that is property to be tamed and claimed. As a result, we have lost touch with the healing, regenerative powers of the natural world and how we are in a symbiotic relationship with it—so much so that we are on a path to global destruction! Reinstating this ancient habit of connecting with the earth and the elements is a part of our collective healing process. Healing the damage we have done to the earth starts on the individual level within each of us.

When I lived by the ocean in Santa Monica, California, I would walk along the shore daily. I would watch the waves go in and out, as a reminder that my emotional state was just like those waves, continuously ebbing and flowing. I would watch storms roll in. I would watch hummingbirds dance in spirals around each other outside my window. I would listen to the crows that seemed to be calling my name. As simple as that sounds, it brought me into greater communion with something larger than myself. I cared about more than just me.

When I am in New York City, I look to the sun. Sometimes it is blazing down; sometimes it's hidden behind clouds. In New York, standing in a pocket of sun in the middle of the winter can be such a treat for my whole being. It reminds me that the winter will indeed be over and everything will be reborn again, as hard and cold as things may seem. Those little moments when I stop on the street and look up and breathe the sun into the depths of my being are everything. They remind me of who I am and why I must find the courage to speak up, to heal, and to share, because the earth also needs my help.

Journaling

Journaling can be part of your daily practice, as mentioned, but it is also a container in and of itself. And there is a reason I've been doing it for so long. Simply put, *because it helps me so much!* When I began the practice way back, it gave me a place to spill my feelings, my fears, my hopes, my insecurities, my dreams. I discovered that getting it all out on paper every morning clears my mind and allows for creativity to flow through me, which feels like a delicious way to start the day.

You don't have to begin with the words "Dear Diary . . ." You can literally just spill your blood, guts, and tears onto a piece of paper as you acknowledge everything that is going on inside you and let it out. I never reread my morning pages unless I am having a supernostalgic moment, packing up an apartment or something like that, and I need to have a good cry. I usually just write it out and let it go.

This container is so simple to create. You can do it on the train, in the bathroom, on vacations, perched on a chair in a crowded bar. Literally *anywhere*. You can even use your phone. The Notes app in my iPhone has probably 10,000 pages on whatever the hell was going on inside me. Letters to lovers I didn't send. Letters to my parents I didn't send. Romantic poetry. Lists and lists of how I was feeling. Mostly to get it out of the mind and onto the page, so my heart feels less heavy, my mind less crowded, and I have a catharsis that feels like a giant breath, a great sigh of relief.

Money

Yes, *money*. Money is a container for you to do what you need to do and have what you need to have. And money is completely related to your spiritual and emotional wellness!

39

I myself used to have a very anarchist approach to money: "Fuck 'the Man'! Money is corrupt!" But the truth is that money is energy. It can be love. It is representative of the time and love I give to you and the time and love you give to me. The fact that we use a small piece of paper (or even just numbers on a digital screen these days) to hold all this energy is hilarious when you think about it. But we need to create a healthy container for the energy of money.

It doesn't mean you need to worship money or create a life that revolves around it, but in order to claim your full power, you have to make peace with money. To find a flow with it and learn how to dance with it. To look at shame, guilt, and inherited beliefs around money and to do the work there as well, so that your money can be a part of your life that holds you and provides support, like your daily practice... or like you taking vitamins!

Otherwise it's just one other area in life where you have friction and where your internal issues get reflected. If you have confidence, self-worth, or self-esteem issues (which may boil down to a lack of self-love), they will show up in your money life. So instead of not including money into our healing and transformational process, we do the opposite: we get close to it.

As we do the work together in this book, money may be an area you want to dig into, and that is *great*. Do not leave it out of your process. Bring it in! Yes, it relates to sex and goddess/divinity and all of it. Let money, and your relationship to it, be a space you heal in, regardless of how much you have. And also a space that can hold you as a container, big or small.

THE ABOVE ARE some of the containers I believe will help you do your work with me, that will keep you healthy and safe as you reclaim your voice and power and body from the tight grips of the tired old systems that are seeking makeovers.

Trust me: by simply putting a few safe containers in place, you will already start to feel a little more secure in yourself and ready to take the risks of healing yourself, claiming your power, sharing your voice. To feel like it's okay to wear that dress that means everybody looks at you. To stand naked in the sun in front of your lover. To create an invention that will help thousands of people suffering from a disease. To deliver the TED Talk. To fall in love. To make loud guttural sounds in bed that are completely bizarre but sexy at the same time. And to step outside of the patterns and ideas you've been fed and be free. To do all of this, you need time. You need space. You need strong-as-fuck containers in place.

GET REAL ABOUT
WHERE YOU ARE AT

I am ready to dive under the surface and into my own depths.

I am ready to reveal my heart, even when it hurts.

I am ready to show up to look at the real shit going on inside me,
   even when it scares me.

Otherwise I'm just going through the motions of life—

Checking things off lists,

Doing what's expected of me,

Working toward goals.

When I show up in the moment and face whatever is truly there,

The masks come down for us all. We can breathe more deeply.

So I am ready to be raw and real.

I am ready to stop people pleasing!

(Stop with empty pleasantries!)

I don't have time for bullshit.

I do have time for whatever truth is itching to be birthed from my soul!

That truth I have time for!

Because if I die before sharing the depth of my real, authentic heart
   with the world,

I would be super bummed.

So here you have my promise.

To show up.

To get real.

To go deep.

BEFORE ANY transformational process begins, we have to start exactly where we are. You may be thinking, "Just get me to the fuck like a goddess part already!" But if it was that easy to skip right ahead to sexy goddess nirvana, then everyone would be doing it. Sure, anyone can *pretend* and put on a show that looks like they are fucking life open and in constant communion with the universe, manifesting this and that. But you just *know* when someone is really bringing something special from a place of authentic realness and depth. You can *feel* a woman who is in her power, sharing her beauty regardless of whether it fits into cultural boxes, expressing her sexuality regardless of the response. When it doesn't matter her size, age, the color of her skin, or how much money she has in the bank.

Across time there have indeed been rule-breaking, paradigm-shifting women who remind me of the myriad ways the goddess/divine/wild cosmos expresses itself through humans. From Joan of Arc to Rosa Parks to Michelle Obama to Sophia Loren to Nina Simone to Frida Kahlo, there are many women out there who have claimed their power, taken major risks, and have a charisma beyond words. There is a *magic* emanating from each of them, and they possess an energy that is mesmerizing.

You've probably thought at some point, "Could I embody *that* much power? That much light? That much radiance? Despite my money issues? My daddy issues? My body image issues? My shyness? Is it really possible for *me* to be a bright, magnetic light, *even with all the shit I've been through?*!"

The answer is, "*Yes*. Fuck yes." It is 100 percent possible. In fact, it is your birthright. And it is not out of your reach.

We all have completely different backgrounds. Different stories we have lived. Each culture brings its own conditioning; each family has its own baggage. Then throw in a media machine that says you get to be a radiant woman only if you get *this* type of bikini wax, work out *that* many days a week, and have hair that looks like *hers*. The list goes on and on, meaning that when it comes to experiencing life as an embodied powerful and magnetic woman, the odds have been stacked against you.

Depending on what cards you've been dealt in this life, the idea of living each day feeling free, beautiful, wild, and connected to yourself and all of creation could feel so out of reach, it's enough to make you want to tear up this book, shake your fists at the sky, or sob in a heap on the floor. (Been there!)

And that is okay. The first and most essential part of your process of returning to your authentic nature is acknowledging where you are at and what you're dealing with. What issues you have in that heavy, heavy suitcase you've been dragging around. It is only from here that we can begin the process of moving beyond feeling like a victim of our life circumstances, to seeing them as *keys* to your becoming the divine expression of *you* that is medicine for the world.

Most people are terrified to unpack their proverbial baggage and meet whatever demons, shadows, and skeletons may be lurking in there. But the truth is, unless you're ready to get really real about where you're at, you will just be putting on a facade—and anything that hasn't been dealt with can creep up at any point to bite you. No amount of makeup, great clothes, or plastic surgery can hide what's festering in that suitcase. People will feel it. Sense it. Smell it.

You may "look amazing," but you won't be magnetic. You won't be truly radiant. Because half of your consciousness, your energy, your presence will still be focused on lugging that heavy suitcase around, leaving you feeling drained, dissatisfied with life, and with a low-level anxiety that doesn't go away.

What are common things we keep in the shadows of this suitcase? Take a moment to think about the things that scare you externally. This could be cancer, war, or being broke. Now take a moment to consider the things that scare you internally. Perhaps it's not being loved, rejection, abandonment, feeling depressed, fear of living a life of anxiety.

Whatever comes up are the surface fears, the obvious ones. The ones our conscious mind has spent time considering and strategizing around, meaning we have adopted ways to consciously try to avoid those things.

The fears we keep in the shadows are the ones we are unconscious of and have perhaps suppressed because they are usually not cute! Seminal psychoanalyst Carl Jung said, "That which we do not bring to consciousness appears in our lives as fate." So even when we pretend these fears are not there, they still show up around us—in lovers, for example, or in horrible bosses. And we wonder, "Why is this happening to me?" Usually it's just these parts of us showing up yet again, asking to be resolved. I've worked with many, many clients to artfully integrate the fears and shadows that are sucking up precious battery power from their operating systems, and the confidence they regain after our work is tremendous!

Jung also posited that "everyone carries a shadow, and the less it is embodied in the individual's conscious life, the blacker and denser it is. . . At all counts, it forms an unconscious snag, thwarting our most well-meant intentions." So, basically, we just can't avoid the tough stuff any longer. We each have healing and transformational work to do, on the individual and collective levels, and just because our ancestors didn't have the time or tools to face the shit doesn't mean we are destined to follow in those footsteps. It's time to show up and speak up and heal.

Any unprocessed pain or trauma that lingers in the darkness of our psyches is always waiting for a moment to pop out. Sometimes it will be triggered to the surface by anxiety about a new lover cheating on us, creating a reaction where we don't open our hearts and instead act withdrawn or defensive. Or we get a new job we really wanted, then spend all our time thinking we don't deserve it and acting nervous and timid with everyone we meet.

The shadowy fears are sneaky. One day you're fine, and then *boom!*, they rise to the surface, leaving you feeling pissed and confused because you finally got the thing you wanted and now these bullshit fears are keeping you locked in anxiety? *Fuck!* You know the feeling or something similar, I am sure. Now you have two choices. You can either try to squish them back down using numbing techniques, like oversnacking, abusing alcohol, overworking, mindless online shopping, overexercising, social media zombifying, too much TV . . . or you can see this as an opportunity to face and *free* that shadow, integrating it into yourself so you feel more whole.

But that is one hell of a scary suitcase to dive into alone. So let's take a peek together.

It could be you've already done years of therapy. If so, bravo! Therapy can help us understand and process so much of our conditioning, our family stuff, and the traumas we've experienced. Finding a therapist who gets you and your shit is amazing. The sliding-scale therapists I found in my midtwenties in Portland, Seattle, and New York City helped me so much. Whether it's via therapy or some other modality of healing, congrats on being a part of the population that is ready to do the work it takes to live a better life and isn't content with checking out with some TV and a bottle of wine when the going gets tough. (Which I have done time and again myself before I had all the tools, so no judgment there!) But whether you've sought therapy to help with a breakup or to help you deal with sexual trauma, low self-worth, money issues, or anything else that is in your suitcases, the fact that you have started to do the healing work is *courageous*! And if you haven't done any *yet* and this is your first foray into healing, then *congrats*! Fuck, it can take a while to get here. I know it. So take a breath and just be assured that this is half the battle.

Let's begin to unpack some of those fears and shadows here and now, bringing awareness to places where our blinders are on, so we can really get to it.

How to Unbrainwash Yourself of All the Bullshit

When we show up to do work on ourselves, we have to remember that we are part of a greater whole. Meaning, we must consider what we have inherited. What beliefs have been ingrained in us by our families. By our religions. By our governments. By the movies. By the magazines.

When I think back to my own childhood, I remember watching *all* the Disney movies. The one about the woman who cracks the heart of the beast open, after he is hella abusive and rude to her. Yes, she sticks around anyway and looks at him like a fixer-upper, which is a pattern I subconsciously repeated for years, starting at age sixteen with my first love, who was arrested about five times while we were together. Still, I kept trying with him because I knew he "had potential." There were quite a few other beastly types over the years... and quite a few other notions that got lodged in my skull from Disney movies.

And then there were the TV shows. Where the girls were pretty and sexy and spent most of their time and money attempting to figure out how to get a man. I saw the same women in the magazine ads—pretty, skinny, blonde, feeling nothing like me. As a young girl, I held myself to thousands, if not millions, of images of beauty standards that I did not fit. Over the years I remember my aunt in Brazil pulling my dad aside and whispering, "What's wrong with her nose? And how about you fix her hair? I know a guy who can fix both." Luckily, my dad didn't listen to them. He just let me walk around as a twelve-year-old with frizzy hair and Umbros in a sea of properly coiffed Brazilian girls. But the notion I was not pretty enough got shoved into me again and again, and chances are it did for you, too.

Each of us has been conditioned. Programmed. Literally *brainwashed* into thinking we are not enough. I am ready for us to revolt and be done with this programming, so we can move on to helping save the planet or creating brilliant inventions and works of art with all the brain and heart power that we have put toward our appearance and self-criticism in the last few hundred years.

Imagine if, as little girls, we had seen images of women of all colors, all nationalities, all shapes, and all sizes in the media. Imagine what the world would be like if we had been taught that beauty was a reflection of how much love and radiance was emanating from a person and not determined by the size of her breasts or waist. I often wonder what life might be like for me as a twenty-first-century woman if I'd been honoring an indigenous female grandmother as my cultural role model instead of supermodels.

But in the West, we got mostly the same one-size-fits-all examples when it came to the kind of women we were told won all the *love*, attention, and success. But perhaps we all know somewhere inside that beauty and the divine feminine come in all shapes, sizes, and colors.

The great thing is that beauty standards are changing fast in many places. More plus-size models grace the runway than ever before, and we see more diversity than there has ever been in magazines and media. But society still has a long way to go, and *we* are a part of that change. Again, as we begin this journey together, it's important to remember that the way we experience love, sex, beauty, and all it means to be a woman has been *programmed into us* and that together we must rewrite those tired old stories and make space for new ones!

And now, with me, with this book, is where you get to *unbrainwash* yourself. From here on in, you get to choose what works for *you* in terms of how you experience, define, and relate to sex, beauty, love, work, the divine, versus all the things that culture, religion, media, or your parents may have chosen for you.

The first step is to become *aware* of all the beliefs that do not belong to us that we've been lugging around. And in order to grow and transform we first have to get really *real*. We have to call out, in ourselves, any old conditioning that is lingering in the backs of our minds. Even if you don't believe on the surface that you have to look a certain way to be loved, if one little part of you, deep in your subconscious, still does hold that thought, then this will remain part of the *you* that you are projecting onto the world.

I'll use some of my story to show you how we do it.

How Much of It Is Your Parents' Shit or Society's Shit?

I was born in Miami in 1984 and moved to Georgia with my mom when my parents got divorced. My dad is from Brazil, and he has been the quintessential guru of my life. But not in the way you might be thinking. In Sanskrit (the language used in yoga, and possibly the oldest language on the planet) *guru* means "that which brings darkness to light"—and since I was five years old, my relationship with my dad has asked me to love and accept myself in ways that seemed impossible at times. All the years when, from my subjective view, I felt abandoned and unloved were actually moments where I had to bring to light my divine nature and learn that I was lovable regardless of another human's love or lack thereof.

And when it comes to conditioning, my spiritual practice has led me to believe that we choose our parents and the circumstance of our childhoods to give us the exact cocktail of lessons that are necessary for our own awakening in this life. This means I do *not* look at myself as a victim of my childhood or trauma. Okay, sure, there are times when I feel like the star of my own personal Italian opera tragedy, but at least 75 percent of the time now I do not. And even when I do, I know how to laugh at myself now and not identify with the story anymore, which is what we'll be doing together as well. I have integrated my stories and allowed them to wake me up and heal me from within. Which has been hard as fuck! A *lot* of deep practice and mind training has gone into not getting stuck in loops about "what I went through as a kid."

My childhood was wonderful and beautiful—and there was what a psychologist would categorize as emotional and psychological abuse. I imagine most humans have experienced such things; we just don't always know it. There was also gaslighting, manipulation, verbal abuse, neglect, abandonment, and indirect sexual abuse, with adults in positions of power sharing about their sex lives with me when I was little, or having sex near me. Again, I could identify these things only after years of working on myself. At the time, it just seemed like regular human stuff. Family drama. No blood was shed, and it didn't seem *that bad*, but later I realized all that stuff had made me feel very unsafe, and I saw how it formed the basis of many other problems that would arise over the years.

My childhood also had a ton of travel and adventure. Many of my summers were spent frolicking in the Brazilian jungle, horseback riding on a cattle ranch, swimming near sharks with my dad in the ocean off the Miami coast, and doing all sorts of other exciting things, externally. But emotionally I felt alone and unsafe and scared during most of it. Being with caregivers who are stuck in their own pain can be weird and confusing when you're a kid. Later, I would be triggered as I lay in the beds of lovers, still feeling unsafe to trust them fully, going into a panic state in my body, sobbing in the dark, wondering if they were going to leave me or if I should leave first, wondering if they were trustable or if I was going to get hurt.

The abandonment I felt from my parents' chaotic and intense divorce, and the way my dad's anger at the world and at my mom and me manifested, would sting in my heart for decades. For example, his teasing me about my weight, saying that I could become fat and therefore unlovable, can't help but have contributed to my eating disorder that emerged at age thirteen and didn't get put to rest until I was thirty. Not his fault, but my own self-defense and desire for love that got confused and wrapped into my self-image over the years.

I now see these as lessons that he gifted me, which, though painful, have made me passionate about helping other women to feel their feelings and feel safe in their bodies, helping people heal from trauma so they don't inflict it on others, and helping people learn to speak up. I have come to see all my life experience as forming the school I chose in this life.

"Trauma" is a word we are hearing more and more, as cultural and collective trauma becomes something that we talk about instead of ignore. The weird thing about trauma is that regardless of the actual experience—whether you were emotionally abandoned by a parent or physically abused, experienced the impacts of war or being involved in a car accident—the trauma can act the *same* in the body and brain. Trauma is what happens as a result of us learning, through our own lived experience, that the world is a dangerous place. That we are no longer safe. That the people on whom we thought we could rely can't actually be trusted. It is not the event itself that causes trauma, but rather the ways in which our lives change shape in the aftermath. Trauma shakes things up in our bodies and our minds, skews our perspectives, warps our realities, and compromises our felt sense of safety. It impacts our ability to discern because it impairs our judgment.

Although many different kinds of events and experiences commonly lead to trauma (sexual assault, physical abuse, natural disaster, war, to name a few), it is important to understand that shared experiences impact individuals in unique ways. That is to say, even if two people experience the same event simultaneously, it is possible for one to move past the occurrence unaffected while the other remains stuck in a trauma response.

So even though someone else's trauma may seem more horrific, more violent, and more aggressive than your trauma of losing someone you love or of being emotionally abused, it may impact your nervous system in the exact same way. There is no clear hierarchy when it comes to pain and how it is stored in our bodies and brains.

This is how *most of us* are walking around in the world. We haven't always stopped to process, to grieve, to rage, to be held, and we may be walking around for years in a posttraumatic state.

Until we stop, drop into our bodies, and start doing the work.

At age twelve, while we were in Lake Tahoe on a ski trip, I learned that my dad had been sexually abused as a child. He pulled over the rental car in Squaw Valley amid mountains of snow and told me: "It's time you knew. I was molested by priests in the Catholic church as a boy. And your mom was sexually abused by a family member as a child." My adolescent mind was blown. I already knew they both dealt with depression and anger, used food and alcohol and romance to cope, and had emotionally intense behavior at times. Now they felt even more unsafe and unstable to the little girl me. I sat in that car not knowing what to say. I had no tools, no support, no one to talk to about it, and I had never felt so alone in my life.

But the dark cloud that was always in the room had been illuminated, which was a relief. What I didn't know then was that when people are unable to face their own pain, they often project it onto us, and sometimes we begin to take it on. As they tell the stories of their traumas, we can also get impacted by them. And so often we assume the role of fixers and holders of space as we attempt to be strong enough for those around us. Which is perhaps one of the main reasons I felt a call to help others heal.

It's more common than we imagine for trauma to get passed down in a family, and that's why it's important we adopt a "the train stops here" mentality. What I mean by this is, we stop passing down the intergenerational wounds and instead do the work to clean them up ourselves, once and for all! *Fuck. Yeah.* A mission that can seem nearly impossible at times, yes. Because the ways we take our parents' shit and redo it, replay it, and regurgitate it onto those we love can be so subtle—imperceptible, almost. For example, we learn how to love from our parents, and so that will be how we attempt to love others, healthy or not. It's a vicious and wild cycle, and the only thing to do is to be the one in *your* family who shows up to do the work, make the magic, and alchemize into the next level!

Since my parents didn't have the tools to deal with their traumas that I have found, they did what they could—ate, drank, looked for love—but ultimately also suffered from anxiety and depression. They found ways to cope with their unhealed pain in order to survive, which I watched from a young age and began to unconsciously model in my own behavior.

My mom did tons of talk therapy, took antidepressants, and is an example of someone who has battled through heavy depression, autoimmune disease, and anxiety, and yet still she has suffered deeply. Very little of her efforts have brought real relief. More recently, she has been exploring deeper work with esketamine therapy, a treatment that was recently made legal with medical supervision, as there are clear results and studies linking this therapy to the relief of PTSD and the depression and anxiety that may arise as symptoms.

Walking alongside her as she has faced it all head on has been an epic example to me of how much courage it takes to heal. The process has not been easy for us both and is a part of why I care so much about this topic.

As a sensitive and empathic kid, I took on a lot of my parents' pain. Psychiatrist Judith Orloff, who has written and taught extensively about empaths, says that "the trademark of an empath is that they feel and absorb other people's emotions and/or physical symptoms because of their high sensitivities. They filter the world through their intuition and have a difficult time intellectualizing their feelings." We may all have this ability, but if our parents were in distress it may be overdeveloped in us, as our childhood will have been spent attempting to parse our own safety and the safety of our caregivers from moment to moment.

If you find yourself taking on other people's feelings and trying to fix and help all the time, you may need some extra work on boundaries. I have been working on this issue for years. As writer Anne Lamott pointed out while I was on a retreat with her and Ram Dass in Hawaii, "Help is the sunny side of control." As kids in households that were out of control, we often become helpers, codependents, or people who are sensitive to others and "know how to fix them."

I grew up an only child with a single mom who had to work full-time while juggling multiple other part-time jobs at night, like baking cakes to sell at her paralegal job and delivering pizzas, so we had enough to pay the bills—all while battling anxiety and depression. So I spent a lot of time alone or worried about her. I felt her struggles. I was mad at her at times, but mostly worried. She sacrificed so much for me and loved me deeply. And yet I still developed my own array of coping mechanisms that weren't always healthy, as I felt for her and missed my father.

I began calorie counting when I was twelve, the same year I joined a gym. I hardened myself to feel safer, which meant I shut down emotionally when I was pretty young, putting my heart behind a shield so it didn't have to get broken again, like it did when my parents divorced. I managed to keep it safe until twenty-nine, when I experienced intense heartbreak for the first time since age five and everything came crumbling down, making me begin to face my own wounding and heal.

Coincidentally, it was also in my preteen years that I felt the call to explore my spirituality and find something inside of me that transcended my pain. My mom was into New Age spirituality and into self-help, and she took me to my first psychic, a man called Bobby Drinnon, who would become my first spiritual teacher and my second father of sorts. He had long white hair and lived on a farm in Tennessee called Rainbow Crest. I was a complex girl with a beautiful, bright soul, and he saw that. He would tell me his dreams about me: that I was carrying rocks around my wrists and ankles, that I needed to work on taking them off so I could fly. He told me I would help others heal one day, and I said, "No way! I wanna be a famous actress!" (I sometimes wonder if all the people who are actors are the people who felt unloved by a parent and are looking for infinite applause and approval that doesn't end. I think that was definitely part of it for me, but Mom also says I just came into this world with something to say.)

But Bobby was right about me getting into the healing arts, even though it felt way less glam than red carpets and champagne-filled parties. It was Bobby who planted the seed in me that there was a mighty energy, a Great Spirit, a source bigger than me, one that ran through all of us. And I believed him because I felt it. I trusted it.

AND SO YOU HAVE the beginnings of both my wounding and my healing journey. The life that, literally, led me here, to this moment, with you.

If I hadn't found the courage to keep showing up to do my work, the patterns of addiction, escape, self-sabotage, scarcity, and coping instilled by my childhood would just have kept playing on repeat in every relationship, and within me, until I died. Maybe they would have carried me through a few divorces, with me wondering why I kept attracting unavailable men. I can see another version of me, bewildered and complaining to my friends over bottles of wine and standing on a scale monitoring my weight into my seventies. But to choose the *opposite*, and to keep showing up to *get real* and look at my shit, has been *the* thing that has brought me to feeling like an embodied goddess, a powerhouse, an eternal spout of wild love, allowing me to transcend my old conditioning and create new patterns. At least on most days, and that is enough.

Of course, you don't have to have had a difficult childhood to need to do healing. "Difficult" is also a relative word. Many of us, regardless of our upbringing, will be familiar with a feeling that we don't belong here. A remembrance of something divine we used to be a part of. Some of us have downright big-ass childhood or adult trauma, or mental or physical health issues, that create inner pain and chaos we need to deal with every day. And sometimes just being here on this planet is hard for our souls. We all have our own obstacles this life. All are opportunities for us to wake up and heal—or else stay sleepwalking through our lives forevermore.

Whatever your recent family history, now imagine this: In your lineage, hundreds of years of repression, depression, angry men, aggressive men, cold and avoidant men, "hysterical" women with zero emotional outlet, perhaps even having been persecuted for their magic and goddess powers. Then *you* appear on the scene, and you take a look at the facts, and you go, "*Hell no, I am not just following these same patterns! I know* it can be better." And so you start showing up like the badass courageous warrior you are.

And here. You. Are.

When you begin to look at all the shit in your suitcase, you might find yourself asking, "Really? You want me to take on being the one to *stop the whole fucking train?* Unpack *all this?!* That's big, baby." But I am here to let you know that it's the most beautiful and noble and generous thing you can do in the world. And that I am so, so proud of you for taking this on and *making art and magic out of it!* It's like you got a pile of shit and with it you are going to become an alchemist and *turn it all into gold.*

You'll see. I did it. You can too.

Depending on what you're dealing with here, it likely will not be easy, but we can find ease in moments. And anyone who says you can just meditate away thousands of years of internalized racism, violence toward women, sexual oppression, or whatever it is you're carrying in your bones—well, I'm sorry, but I give you full permission to throw a kale smoothie in their face.

Healing deep-seated intergenerational wounds is a *process.* One with many layers and crazy ups and downs. As you open the doors to the deepest parts of yourself, the butterflies will emerge ... along with the moths, the boogeymen, the ghosts of Christmas past, and all the things you didn't know you had the courage to face.

One of my dearest friends, Ruby Warrington, author and visionary thought leader (whom I have a lot of matching baggage with), once said: "Do not fear your feelings, for they are lighting the path to your full presence and your formidable power." It particularly resonates with me because it's true. The path to learning to fuck like a goddess is one that first requires deep work. Showing up. Feeling it all. Getting real. If it was easy and glam, everyone would be doing it!

There are many things that may be preventing you from living as *full-power you.* A time your parent said you weren't good enough that hit your heart hard. Living in the shadow of your talented, confident sibling. Someone calling you fat. Physical, mental, or emotional abuse. Or you battling an autoimmune disease. So many things can contribute to an internal world of pain, confusion, anxiety, and depression, and we can either put on a happy face, pour a glass of wine, and keep on marching through life, or we can stop and unpack what's going on and process and deal with *what has happened.*

If we don't stop and discuss that which has happened, then we are avoiding it! Because racism has happened. Rapes. The genocides of indigenous peoples. And so much more—in our own stories and in our collective history. And it is *ours* to unpack. First, we must get to work creating an inner landscape of emotional and spiritual well-being. Turning, again and again, to the inner light of who we *truly* are, as we overcome the pain and beliefs and patterns keeping us small and we begin to sit and talk and get real about everything that has happened.

It takes courage, stamina, and epic levels of self-care, and I know you can do it. Remember, you are not alone in this journey. Thousands, perhaps millions, of people are waking up, standing up, protesting the status quo, looking at their sexual traumas, their internalized racism and privilege, and beginning to unwind the years and years of pain and suffering laced into their DNA and settled beneath their skins. It's a beautiful time to be a human on this planet and to be walking this path for the generations to come.

THE TRANSFORMATIONAL WORK: CULTIVATING AWARENESS

Know Your Blocks

Okay, let's get real and identify what is preventing you from going *full-power you*. This means looking at the shit you deal with in the day to day and tracing it back to the conditioning you received. For example, since I grew up never knowing when I would see my dad, I have had a lot of fears around trusting men and receiving their love. So at the core of a lot of the issues I have experienced in my life is this issue of trust—wondering if I can truly open to people and if I can let them love me. This core issue has been present in my friendships, in my work life, with my clients, and especially with love relationships, where I have felt like I can handle myself and my problems on my own and so have not let people into my heart. Which has meant isolation, loneliness, and a lack of love from others, until I dealt with the wound directly.

I also grew up with a feast-or-famine mentality around money. If we had it, Mom would spend it on her and me, treating us to a dinner or something special, but then we would be nervous about having enough money to buy gas so Mom could get to work or pay the electricity bills. So nowadays I have to watch myself with this pattern. It doesn't rule me, but it pops up here and again—which is where having my money container helps me. I have a savings account. I make budgets. And I remove the possibility for over-spending or being blind to the truth of my finances. This took *ages* for me to conquer, though. And it is an ongoing practice.

What are your blocks to unleashing your full magic? You will find them in *the places you get triggered*. They are *essential* to notice without shame or judgment, but simply with awareness.

Start to notice what being triggered feels like to you. For me, I get this "Maybe I'm gonna cry" feeling behind my eyes or pressure in my chest, coupled with an overall heaviness in my limbs and a thought that says: "You need to be alone. You should probably leave." But leaving or checking out is not always the answer. Now, I can recognize that thought as coming from the scared five-year-old me, and I can remind her she is okay.

I want you to begin by writing down where you get triggered. If you begin to notice the exact moment you start to get all funky and sink into your wound, you can understand how to come in and intervene before you slide all the way back into it. When are you most triggered? Scrolling through Instagram? At work? While reading *Vogue*? When you talk to Mom?

You can write a short paragraph for each question below, or a sentence, and if you want to write more, more power to you. Remember, this is all about you checking in with yourself to get real and become aware of where you are and what is holding you back—so you can learn to make love to your life like the divine being you are.

- What pisses you off, makes your blood boil, and makes heat rise in your system? What people? Images? Situations?

- What makes you super sad? Again, what people? Images? Situations?

- What do you hate or feel ashamed of about yourself? Admit the hard stuff.

- What's your relationship with your mom like? Currently and as a child.

- What's your relationship with your dad like?
  Currently and as a child.

- What's your relationship with your siblings like?
  Currently and as a child.

- What area of your life do you feel at a standstill in? Stuck?
  An area where you are trying to grow or to break free of but you "can't."

- What is your current relationship to sex like?
  (We will go deep on this later, but begin here!)

- Your current relationship to your body?

- To love and romance?

- To your mission and purpose?

- To being seen?

- To receiving love?

- To giving love?

- When do you feel the most alive?

- When do you feel the most joyful?

- When do you feel the most loved?

- When do you feel the most like a goddess?

- When do you feel the most sexy?

We're going to stop there for now. This is an extensive yet simple inventory that will serve as a road map of all the places you may be hiding some *blocks* to your magic. If some big stuff came up, don't worry—we will go deeper into how to work with your blocks and shadows later on.

Move Past Resistance

As I mentioned earlier, you may encounter *massive* resistance as you do the work in this book. You may lose the book, hide the book, throw the book away, burn it in a funeral pyre. You may be pissed at this book. You may also get pissed at me!

This is normal. As you are transforming, your fear mechanism may come in and try and sabotage this process. You also may get foggy, distracted, dissociated, want to look at your phone, want to eat anything in sight. All these things are *super* common ways we limit our own growth without even knowing it. Our fear mind actually does it to try to keep us safe. Because if we stay where we are, at least it knows we can survive there!

And fear is *crafty as hell.* From here on, any time your fear comes in, I want you to name it. Find out what age it is. I mean, literally, ask it: "At what age did you, this fear, take root in me?" Notice if it's related to something from your early childhood, teen years, or even last week. And then say to the fear: "Dear Fear, I really appreciate you trying to keep me alive. *Really!* But the truth is, I am 100 percent ready to rise. To transform. To live a grand and beautiful life. To be seen. To shine. And I promise I will take care of myself in the process. If you try to prevent me from shining every time I take a step, I will never grow."

And treat it all with the utmost compassion. With kindness. A loving inner voice goes a long way when we do this work. You can be annoyed and angry and sad when you realize how much fear is sabotaging your process, or you can approach it with love. It's a choice.

So that you can begin when fear is making resistance creep in, I want you to consider:

- When has fear sabotaged you from growth?

- From speaking up?

- From saying hello to someone you've wanted to meet your whole life?

- From helping or defending someone in need?

- From telling someone you loved them?

- From wearing that amazing dress you already bought and look great in? (Maybe so great your fear is of making other people jealous?!)

Write a few lines in your journal for each of the above questions.

Guess what? Fear actually does a great job of alerting us when it's time to pay attention. To become *aware*. The key is not to let it take over. So when fear (or its sister, resistance) pops up, here are some ways to combat it and *get present* in your day to day. You will want to refer back to this page, I promise! Screenshot it, bookmark it, and keep it close!

Ways to Move Past Fear and Stay Open So You Can Grow

There are many ways we can quickly move past a fear response before it overtakes us. Here are a few of my favorite techniques and practices that I use throughout my day, again and again, whenever I have fear thoughts or responses in my body.

- When the mind takes over with its stories and reasons why you should play small, take a deep, yummy, big breath into your lower belly. When fear comes, it will try to shut everything down: love, speaking up, being seen . . . It feels out of control and makes you small. Your mind becomes tiny and tight. A deep belly breath with an audible sigh will change this in a very short period of time. It may take a bit of practice, but this is an essential practice to help you arrive back to your fullness.

- Shake the resistance out of your body. Literally! Shake your hands. Shake your arms. Shake your legs.

- Dance for five minutes to one of your favorite songs.

- Exercise. Move the fear and resistance out of your body with a quick jog or some jumping jacks. Do this if you need something more hardcore than just shaking or dancing to break through the resistance wall. Sometimes exercise can become an escape, though, so watch that you aren't using working out to avoid looking at yourself deeply. (I used to avoid feelings in this way *a lot!*)

- Scream! I will actually ask you to scream a lot throughout this book. Screaming is cathartic—it's a release. Sometimes when we hit a wall, a good scream is needed to get it out! You can also scream into a pillow or into the water in the bathtub. It will allow a physical release in the body, which will also create a physiological nervous system reset.

- Self-pleasure. Consciously taking a moment to create pleasure in your body, sensually or sexually. When entering into this space, remember: this is not an escape into a quick pleasure burst, but instead a way to get present. Very tricky discernment! Rubbing one out real quick may not be the medicine to combat fear. But getting present and breathing as you touch yourself can get you out of your head and back into your body in a beautiful way. (I have a whole section on this art later on.)

- Reframe. When fear comes, zoom out and think about your grandmothers, your future kids, the girls in the world who don't have the freedom you do. Remind yourself that as you grow and expand, you are doing it for everyone who couldn't, for those who can't, and to pave the way for those to come. For example, if I get through *my* body shame, then perhaps my future daughter won't have to deal with it because I will be a positive example for her.

Bottom line: When fear comes to visit, do not let it set up shop in you for the day or week. Try the practices above and stay in the sweet spot of change, as uncomfortable as it may be.

Add your own ideas to this list and put it on your bed stand, in your sacred space, near your mirror, or wherever you will see it daily, so it will be there to help you any time you encounter a block. Know that you may need to do a few things on this list before you get clear again. And that is okay.

With this new sense of self-awareness, we can move forward with turning any blocks you have into *fuel* that shoots you to the moon, expands your power, frees your voice, and lets your radiance *shine* in the world. It takes courage to acknowledge the fears and bullshit weighing you down, so take a moment and please do a victory dance, scream from your belly, or laugh loudly! This is the first step to change.

Next, let's face the fears and blocks together and commit to not ignoring them or pretending they aren't there. Let's make art out of them. Let's walk into the fire together and come out the other side like a motherfucking phoenix.

HOW TO HEAL YOUR SHIT

My healing is my sacred art.
Transforming my shit into gold is the ancient alchemical way laced into
my DNA.
It is buried within my bones, this ancient wisdom of self-regeneration
that I seem to have "forgotten."
But I have not forgotten.
This art is indeed within my reach.

Like trees that drop leaves and grow more again, I will shed.
Like forests that regrow after a fire, I will be reborn.

I know I have spots in me that need to be razed, cleared,
transformed, awakened.

I am no longer afraid of these tender spots.
I see them as vaults of power, waiting to be awakened.

As stories, waiting to be told.
As art, waiting to be created.

I will show up.
I will dare to open,
Put the time in, and turn it all into gold.

CONGRATS ON GETTING HERE. You have already completed the hardest step: becoming *aware* of all that is preventing you from showing up, being present, being radiant, receiving love, and fucking like a goddess. This takes radical responsibility and courage, and it is usually where most people stop. It can be completely overwhelming to even look at our demons, our traumas, the dark parts, the sad parts, and anything else that has been kept in the shadows. Because they hurt. Because they are "shameful." Because they are often culturally unacceptable. It feels way easier to hide them all away behind busy schedules, plastic surgery, makeup, and wine. But these hidden, unhealed wounds are what turn into anxiety, depression, eating disorders, and disease. They are what keep you from living a life of love, presence, and purpose.

The rest of the work we do together won't always be easy, but it can also be fun, silly, joyful, and empowering as *fuck*. Now that you have noticed and become aware of the hand of cards you are working with, so to speak, everything and anything is possible.

The next step on your transformational journey toward you claiming your full power and voice is *uprooting* the deeply seated beliefs so they are no longer running your inner operating system. When you are stuck in limiting beliefs and fears, it's like you have too many apps going. The "I am not good enough" app is competing with the "My voice is not worthy" app, which in turn is vying with the "Am I lovable?" app. All these stories are running your battery down! Not to mention taking up tons of mental space throughout the layers of the mind. The "Am I lovable?" app alone is replaying the evidence *all the time*: "Remember, so-and-so dumped you, and Dad never hugged you, and that one friend ghosted you . . ." With all this going on behind the scenes, how are you supposed to have the energy to show up for the life of your dreams?

And some of these programs have been running for *years*, going back generations in your family. Now it's up to you to say, "Enough is enough! I am ready to break free of these old-ass stories. I am ready to create *new* stories and *new* evidence about my life and myself."

In this section, I am going to walk you through the way I have graduated from my own blocks and helped clients and students to use painful feelings as fuel, as catalysts for change and healing. My methods are based on lived experience, ancient tantric practices, and learning the art of self-transformation and internal alchemy with plant medicines—healing that encompasses the body, the heart, and the mind as one.

I've broken it all down into simple steps for you.

The Process: Steps to Embodied Transformation

When something painful or tough or triggering comes up, this is what we do: first, we *stop*. We *feel*. If we avoid it or don't feel it fully, it will return even more powerfully. So we *dive in* . . .

1 **Feel it.** We use the practice of embodiment to drop into the heart and body—by which I mean both the gross (physical) body *and* the subtle (energetic) body. This means using breath, sounds, and slow movements to literally feel the blocks, the anxieties, and the pains in the body so we can heal and trans-

form them. *How?* Start by getting out of your head and *breathing into your belly.*

I first began this practice in acting school when a teacher told me to make the sound "HA" really loud and soften my belly after years of holding it in. She made me do it until I cried— sobbed violently, actually! All the feelings stuck in my body began to flow. I came out of my head and into my belly, and my life started again in some ways. "HA" is actually a bij mantra, or seed syllable, in Sanskrit and is used in various tantric, yogic, and Buddhist traditions, though I did not know that at age eighteen, when I began!

I have now led a practice influenced by this that I call "How to Embody Your Feminine Fire"—a combination of breath work, sound and vocal work, and movement—for *thousands* of women. I've gotten email after email saying, "This changed my life!" *Feeling*: it's the first step in healing.

2 **Identify it.** After we dive into the feeling, we are just *beginning* to do the transformational internal alchemy. Next, we stop, we breathe normally *in the belly*, and we ask ourselves: "Where is this feeling or block primarily in my body? What is this feeling like in color, texture, temperature? Is there an image associated with it?" (Example: "My anxiety feels like tight rubber bands around my heart and gray static behind my eyes.") Then ask yourself: "How old is this feeling? When did I first feel this?" (Some of our blocks are *old!*) Allow a memory or a belief to come forth. Emphasis on *allow*—don't force.

3 **Magnify it.** Now that we know what is going on and where it is coming from, we feel the feelings associated with the memory or belief *fully*. We go in even deeper than before! With loud "HA's"!

Sighs! Moans! *Deep* breaths! Until it feels almost unbearable! We use breath and sound to bring the feelings to their full magnitude.

This is not the same as reliving past traumas, but rather allowing the body to speak to us in the present and open the places where we are blocked. Since now we have a memory or a belief attached—now we know where they are from—the feelings from step 1 ("Feel it") naturally get bigger. When we work with emotions, we ride the energy like waves. We do not attach to them or identify with them; we allow them to transform us from the inside by using *big breaths*. To carve us out and drop us in more deeply into ourselves. We use sighs, moans, and growls to facilitate a *release* until we *pop* into awakening and clarity and more aliveness. It is good to give thirty to forty-five minutes to this practice. An hour is even better. (The process up to here may have to be repeated multiple times before a memory, emotion, or block is ready to be fully cleared, and that is okay.)

4 **Heal it.** Once the feeling has been fully felt, we bring our breath back to a calm pace; we feel into the present, into what has shifted in us; and we can visualize putting that part of our child self or past self to rest. The part of us that was not able to fully process the event or feeling at its inception gets a proper moment to be heard, witnessed, held, and set free if it needs to be. Then we can rest in the completion, enjoying the opening and the space that was created. This is the power of visualization. And it is ancient and fast!

5 **Release it.** Finally, we feel ourselves in the here and now, no longer identified with the old memory or belief but instead noticing how we feel after this internal alchemical transmutation of feeling into awakening. We allow ourselves to

emerge, feeling lighter and more free. We can feel into who we are now, without that old block or fear driving our system; but instead it has been loved, expressed, and released. We find ourselves back at center. We breathe.

That's the way we begin to make change, using the tools at our disposal: breath, sound, feelings, visioning. And we allow our pain to open us, instead of close us. To wake us up to the present! We alchemize.

In Western society, when addressing mental or emotional pain, we often go straight to talk therapy or rationalizing things in the mind, which is an important part of the picture, but I believe it can take us only so far in the healing process. Using this visceral, *embodied* process to dive into my deepest, most embedded wounds is how I have healed them. I've seen it work for hundreds of other women in my sessions and retreats, too! In fact, I believe so strongly that *this* is how we really heal from deep, old, sticky traumas and generational wounds that embodied healing has become my heart's calling in this latest phase of my life.

Because I am so passionate about embodied healing, sexual healing, and healing around the female body, I developed a six-month program a few years ago dedicated to this study and process. Each month, for a group of clients, I curated a different experience of various embodied modalities that have been life changing for me. Members of the group were working with healing around disordered eating, addictions to pills, bulimia, PTSD from being the victim of attempted murder, PTSD from rape, PTSD from childhood sexual abuse and kidnapping, and PTSD from sex work.

At the beginning of our time together, we worked with a female healer in a ceremony with the powerful visionary plant medicine ayahuasca. Ayahuasca has been used by many indigenous peoples for thousands of years in the Amazon jungle area, and is recently becoming a widespread spiritual go-to in the Western spiritual world, touted as a medicine that brings what many people describe as "five years of therapy in one night."

We also participated in Japanese rope-bondage suspensions, shamanic breath work, polarity and intimacy work, and a snake dancing ceremony. Ancient, powerful healing tools brought to us by healers trained in these arts.

And for our last experience, we worked with psilocybin-containing magic mushrooms, brought to American culture in 1957 via an article in *LIFE* magazine by ethnomycologist R. Gordon Wasson after his visit to the Mazatec healer María Sabina in southern Mexico. Evidence of mushrooms being used by humans dates back to 9000 BCE. Mushrooms and ayahuasca have been a very powerful part of my own healing process, which I have translated and applied to my teachings here. (For more on ayahuasca and mushrooms and the traditions they come from, please see my reading recommendations on alexandraroxo.com/flag.)

As they had for me, the practices and modalities in this program of embodied healing truly worked for the group as well. Each member of our group emerged as completely new. Starting businesses, dedicating their lives to service, speaking up. It was a return to the earth, the body, the plants, and connection as medicine—and that exploration has formed the basis of what I will teach you in this chapter. My journey working with these perhaps more extreme modalities and tools has allowed me to find the wisdom and teachings that I can bring to you in a more practical way.

So don't worry, no actual psychedelics or dancing with snakes is required for this book. While everything I am going to guide you through is influenced by and rooted in those ancient wisdoms, it is all simple and safe enough for you to do at home.

So, this is where we dive into the tough shit and alchemize the pain into power.

But first let's talk about *fear*, so that it doesn't stop you from having the courage to dive in.

From Preprogrammed Mode into Cocreation Mode

Often, the ways the traumas and hurts of our past stick with us mean our default operating system is running on fear. This is completely understandable and totally normal. Here is what happens:

1 You arrive on earth as a beautiful, loving baby.

2 You get hurt and arrive into family patterns and collective issues.

3 You shut down parts of yourself in order to not get hurt again and to cope with the scene you got dropped into. Your system forms patterns based on preventing pain. From then on you operate out of closure, defense, and self-protection.

Okay, it's more complex than that, but at the same time it is that simple. When we experience things that scare us and cause us pain, they make an imprint and create a fear in us of experiencing such things again. Imagine sweet baby you: open, innocent, and ready to experience the world. Then you get told you aren't good enough. You learn that you're only lovable if you do or are A, B, or C. Perhaps you get taken advantage of, or you undergo any series of traumatic events. Your nervous system, and the fear you feel, will do whatever it takes to avoid that happening again *at all costs*! And this is where you unconsciously start creating blocks to your internal creative flow. The love shuts down. The life-force energy. The radiance. This can happen fast or else subtly over time.

We are smart creatures, and staying safe is beneficial to our survival. However, it can also prevent us from loving, being loved, speaking up, and living in our full divine freedom. When we become aware of the blocks that we have unconsciously created, there comes a point when we need to tell our bodies, our beings, and our nervous systems: "I've got you. It is safe now to open up beyond this hurt." Otherwise, we block love without knowing it. We block success and wonder why it is not coming. We protect our bodies with layers of extra weight and don't know why it's not going away. We do all kinds of things to protect our sweet selves from *ever* having to go through the things we went through again. And the weirdest part is, most of it is subconscious. We don't even know we are doing it!

In order to reclaim your full power and your full potential, all parts of you have to come back online. Nothing can be living in a paralyzed state of fear. This will take time, but slowly you will thaw, soften, and begin to trust life and yourself again.

This is when you move from living from fear-based programing to cocreating a new way of living and being with the divine. From here, you get to decide exactly how *you* want to live. How open, how free, how joyful, and how alive you want to feel each day. You are no longer simply letting your past experience dictate your levels of happiness today.

It may sound obvious, but look at an *authentically* peaceful person. Or an *authentically* joyful person. One whose heart you can truly feel beaming through their entire existence. They have somehow managed to love and laugh in ways that are bigger than their fears and their traumas. Maybe they didn't have a fucked-up childhood in this lifetime, and maybe they did. This is not about comparing who supposedly "had it worse"—we've all experienced trauma on some level. But try to feel into the heart of this joyful person for a moment. Somehow, they have managed to override the fear and have chosen to stay vulnerable, hopeful, and open anyway to life, despite the fact that they may get hurt again. It's a bold choice. A risky one. But it is *this* choice that brings bliss beyond our wildest dreams.

Working to rewrite our fear-based programing doesn't mean we are going to erase the pains of the past. They will never go away completely, but we can find ways to integrate them and stop letting them dictate our life experience. This happens when we can *accept* their teachings and lessons—when we allow those hurts to make us the colorful, complex goddesses we are. This shift will go on to inform our work in the world. And then we keep opening to the joys of life. We no longer feel like we have to spend our whole lives hiding. We take a stand. We shout. We dance wildly! *This* is the transmutation of our traumas into gold.

I spent years trying every modality I could find to help me get past my fears and heal. I sat quietly in meditation. I pushed my stories back and forth in talk therapy. But it wasn't until I found *embodied* ways of healing that I began to face my childhood wounds, put to rest my disordered eating, dealt with my sexual trauma, and could stop using booze, sex, or love to escape. It's also when I started to deal with the flood of feelings I had suppressed with busyness, wine, exercise, and all the other crafty things I had used to avoid looking into my heart.

Western approaches to healing are often suppressive: "anti"-depressant, "anti"-pain, and "anti"-anxiety meds, designed to address the symptoms and not causes. For me, a return to the earth and the body was so key, along with therapies and practices that were designed to evoke an even *deeper* exploration of my pain.

The earth is full of medicine for us. From the beans of coffee to those of cacao, so much of what we consume for fuel, medicine, or pleasure is derived from plants that come from the earth. Unfortunately, many plants, and many traditions and cultures that they came from, have been greatly capitalized on and exploited, and this conversation is a complex one that I enter into with great care, reverence, respect, knowledge, and discernment to avoid causing further exploitation or appropriation. Take cacao, for instance, a plant native to the Amazon basin and used in ceremonies and rituals for more than four thousand years. It was exported to Europe in the seventeenth century, and the mass production of it occurred over time. Now cacao is often diluted with large amounts of sugar by large corporations to sell as "chocolate," a product very far removed from cacao's original form, roots, and sacredness. This is not a bad thing per se, simply complex, and also beyond the scope of this book to explore deeply.

My healing work with plant medicines like peyote and ayahuasca and psilocybin asked me to sit in my internal wounds and reminded me that I had the courage within me to face my toughest experiences and fears head on. By the grace of many indigenous peoples sharing their healing tools with me, I was able to moan and cry and sweat and go *into* the fears and pains as opposed to avoiding them. I learned that this was the only way to release them and truly heal. The deep honor and gratitude I have in my heart for these invitations is beyond words.

When I was invited to my first plant medicine ceremony, my mind was alight with fears, such as: "What if I lose my mind? What if I'm taken advantage of? Are these people legit? Is this in integrity?" And on another level, a part of my soul *knew* there was deep medicine there for me. I felt a full-body *yes*; even in fear, it was simply a *yes*.

As I sat with the brew of ayahuasca, I had some of the most profound healings of my life. I heard a voice inside me say: "You have been living in ego. It is time to dedicate your life to service." This was the moment my career as a filmmaker came to a turn, and I went through a few years of deep healing with my own shadows and transitioning into a life of deeper service. I listened to the medicine. I started a new chapter. I devoted myself to sharing my heart openly, even when it was hard. And here I am.

I am fully aware of the atrocities toward indigenous peoples throughout history and in current times, so as a white woman to have a hand extended to me by being invited into traditional ayahuasca ceremonies, sweat lodges, and peyote ceremonies over many years has been life changing in itself. This is an example of the kind of openhearted invitation into healing processes that my own Western culture doesn't really offer. It has been a generosity that has deeply touched my heart and has inspired me to step into greater responsibility and accountability.

Sitting in sacred ceremonies over the last fifteen years with native elders and peoples, with the plant teachers or in sweat lodges or with cacao, has profoundly impacted me. Their reverence for the earth, their faith in the healing power of her medicines, and their generosity have opened me in major ways. I was accepted and honored, and in those spaces I cried, and I purged, and I healed. The medicine of ayahuasca and the indigenous master healers who are sharing it with Westerners like myself are changing our reality, and my hope is that as these medicines become more widespread they are treated with the honor and respect they are due.

My experience with plant medicines is that they powerfully clean the heart, the spirit, and the body. Through trusting a master plant, I experienced a medicine of the earth, from the earth, ancient, and very clear to the source of creation, from nature. This path is not for everyone, though. It is complex, it can be dangerous, and it requires treading with caution. Like anything, the plant medicine space has charlatans, untrained people claiming to be shamans, and people with harmful intentions. I recommend several books and resources on this topic on my website so that if do you feel called to this path you may enter it safely and with care. And because it is not for everyone, I have translated many teachings from my own journeys here for you to access and use without taking any plant medicines.

And so, my life is an ongoing spiritual quest. I have experimented and tried various embodied healing and spiritual practices—ones that I like to think of as feminine, ones that go beyond the rational mind, ones that defy explanation—on behalf of my own healing and to see what I might bring to my clients and other people.

Another avenue where I experienced great healing was with conscious kink—exploring sexual shadows, fetishes, and desires with intention and awareness. I have played out feelings and scenarios I was scared of, I have engaged in power dynamics that scared me, and I have been tied up and suspended from ceilings by an incredible female rope healer and teacher named Blue, as a way to feel my own power again, to heal and reclaim my sexuality and my body, and to release the collective sexual shadows I had inherited and participated in.

I also was initiated into and studied several Tibetan Vajrayana tantric Buddhist practices, including the study of a practice named Feeding Your Demons from teacher Lama Tsultrim Allione. In this practice, which she outlines in her book by the same name, you imagine feeding yourself to your personal demons, and you turn them into allies. This helps transform the parts of you that you most hate and most fear into parts that actually enliven and empower you. It has been liberating for me to explore this ancient wisdom, so aligned with the other practices I have studied.

I also danced with snakes in ceremony for a few years with a powerful priestess. As the serpents wrapped themselves around me, they squeezed me like healers going directly to all my energetic wounds. I cried, and as odd as it may sound, they helped me release emotions and fears stored in my cells, in my tissues. Afterward I felt stronger and more open to love than ever.

And after all this exploration and study, I have learned how to adapt what I've learned in those deep spaces for any person wishing to heal. I've learned that healing and transformation happen in the present, in the body, by facing and feeling our fears—which can be done in the simplest of ways, with breath, presence, awareness, and listening to the heart.

Even without snakes and plant medicines, the art of self-healing and transformation requires courage, and it requires you to go beyond the comfort zone of fear that your body created to protect itself—but not everyone has to go to the extremes (as I love to do) in order to heal and learn.

Why Talking about Your Shit Is Not Enough

With my clients and in my own life, I have witnessed time and again how transformation works. But just as no two humans are alike, no two paths to reclaiming our full selves and doing the healing will ever be the same. I had to look all over the place until I found the practices that really worked for me. As with many people, it began with talk therapy. But, luckily for me, as a nontraditional gal, I was not in traditional therapy.

While I was living in Portland, Oregon, after leaving New York University, I found a sliding-scale therapist who combined mindfulness, Buddhism, and Western psychotherapy. I went into her office and told her, "Hi. I've never had an orgasm with a partner—maybe this is because I was raped—and I want to work through that." I was twenty-two. I think I paid her twenty dollars an hour (whatever the amount, it was a lot for me at the time on my barista salary). And so for weeks we worked through my sexual history together, talking through every experience that had affected the way I orgasm and how safe I felt to let go.

We talked through my experience of being raped, and we also wrote a list of all the people I had slept with or engaged with sexually, and we felt into how each had felt and was still feeling in my body. What shame was there. What pain was there. Where I was still embarrassed. Where I had not said no loudly enough and was still ashamed. Heather, my therapist, helped me to see that every little pocket of shame and anger at myself or those who hurt me was keeping me from letting go into my orgasms with the man I was now in love with. I had already gone to school for playwriting, theater, and film, and though I knew that writing and storytelling were essential parts of the healing process, I had almost overlooked the fact I could use these modalities personally. Now, almost fifteen years later, storytelling and owning your story and feelings are an *essential* part of how I heal and lead others to heal. If you've buried or denied or hidden your stories away, then you will have to accept them and look at them before you can transform them. And that is what I did with Heather.

But here's where we took it into the body and not just the mind. After looking at my sexual stories one by one, we came up with a plan that included my self-pleasuring with my boyfriend in an attempt to feel safe to let go in front of him. I was nervous, but I did it. He held me, and we were in the bathtub, lit by candles. And, with practice, it became way easier for me to orgasm with a partner. What I learned was that because the control and tightness and fear of letting go were manifesting *in my body*, I had to find a way to show my body it was safe to let go. Because it was *my body*, not my mind, that was still living in the past and in fear. Looking back, I see this may have been my first step toward fucking like a goddess— meaning owning my stories, even the painful ones, and releasing the shame and guilt and fear in my body in order to be present and enjoy my life.

I was so lucky to find Heather. Often a lot of talk therapy focuses mainly on the mind, on pushing a story back and forth without you always knowing where to take it, but my work with her showed me it is essential to add practices and techniques to the talk therapy that help open my heart and my body as well. Thankfully, many therapists nowadays are doing work that also includes the body.

And you do not need thousands of dollars to do this work. The idea that therapeutic work is expensive is an illusion and an excuse. (Remember what I said about resistance and the ways our brain tries to sabotage our attempts to grow?) There are plenty of sliding-scale therapists out there, and what I am teaching you in this book, which is essentially a self-healing process that incorporates many of the techniques I have experienced over the years, is *free* (besides the cost of the book, of course). We are using the power of writing, breath, sound, sharing, and our bodies to heal. All of which have been available to humans since the beginning of time.

Generational Stuff: The Baggage You Were Gifted

Remember how we learned that a lot of our shit (pain, patterns, fears, traumas) is actually passed down from our parents or care-givers? They likely handed down their genetics to us, and, like it or not, they also instilled in us our core values and beliefs. They taught us how to give and receive love. They taught us what safety looks and feels like. And, as discussed, they will have also passed down their traumas. This makes them our first and most complex teachers—or gurus—on this planet.

You may be adopted. You may only have one parent. You will have your own story. But our nervous systems calibrate from the way our primary childhood caregivers teach us, love us, talk to us, et cetera. This creates the patterns for *all* relationships in our lifetime. For what we find and accept as "normal" when it comes to touch, love, affection, or sharing—patterns that play out with everyone we meet.

Once I understood my own inherited issues—growing up with parents who had early childhood trauma, some addiction strug-gles, deep depression—I realized *so much* about myself and why I became the person I am. Why I had IBS and menstrual issues. Why I developed workaholic and overachieving tendencies. Why I shied away from deep intimacy and trusting people. Why I pre-ferred to do my own thing rather than depend on or ask anyone for help.

These last two are examples of the fallout from the abandonment wound I got from my childhood, which is something I have sat with in my own healing again and again.

The fact that my parents were flight attendants when I was in my early years meant I was left with strangers a lot. Nannies. Au pairs. Women who were kind but who could never love me like a parent.

Those summers with my dad in Brazil, he would often take me to a friend's cattle farm and drop me with a family who had kids my age for a few weeks. I didn't know anyone there. I was afraid. There I was, age six or seven, in the middle of a foreign country, with no way to contact my parents. I experienced the feeling of being abandoned again and again at a very young age. Learning how to get by on my own meant learning how to shut off my emotions and go into survival mode.

The abandonment and rejection wounds that were the result of this were triggered any time a friend or lover didn't call me back for a few days, for example. A leaden weight would come over my arms, a fuzziness would gather behind my eyes, and my heart would shrivel and hide. I couldn't feel the magic in music or food. Because of my bodily response, I knew my wound was being activated. But once I fully understood that this was part of my conditioning, I was able to go further and develop a sense of compassion for myself. And now my abandonment wound has transformed into something else, a gift of knowing love within me, a love that no one can reject but me.

This has meant working through a lot of feelings aimed at my parents. This part took *years*! I had to journal about it. Cry about it. Make art about it. Purge it in plant medicine ceremonies. Until finally I was able to accept that it is part of what makes me me. And that I love me, wounds and all. This takes time. It's an art. It also becomes a soft place where love finds you. As the Sufi poet Rumi said: "The wound is the place where light enters you." As much as it sucks to feel the pain when the wounds come back up, each time they do, it is an opportunity to dance with depth, with feeling, and with the divine. To love and open anyway. Each time you feel the old pain, breathe into it instead of trying to avoid it, or fear it, or fix it—and it will shift, you'll see. It will be uncomfortable at times, but sitting in the fires will strengthen you and help you to blossom in ways nothing else can.

Remember, becoming *aware* of these patterns in the first step. We do this with meditation, slowing down, writing, sharing, and story-telling. We check out the past, assess, and come back to the present.

Then we physically *feel* into the imprint the wounds have left in our emotional and physical bodies. We use breath and sound to get into these wounds and blocks.

We *identify* the core wound, belief, block, or pattern that we are healing and transforming. Where did it come from? What is our name for it?

We *magnify* the feeling until we are completely in it.

And this is when we *heal* the wound or block, by accepting it, for-giving it, and integrating it, until we are finally able to *release* the struggle around it and simply let it be. This is the purification of our karma. The letting go. The opening.

I know this sounds intense. Working through this process is not always cute and can often feel heavy, sticky, frustrating, and even embarrassing! But it can literally be done as a practice in ten-minute increments in your car. Or you can set aside some time in your sacred space and make it a two-hour practice on a Saturday morning. And remember, some blocks may take time

So be patient! If it's a deep one, just keep at it, until one day you will feel complete. I promise. You will feel like it's taught you all you needed to learn and can now be recycled into a source of power and joy. This is the inner alchemy of turning your shit into gold.

THE TRANSFORMATIONAL WORK: "FEEL IT TO HEAL IT"

"Feel it to heal it" is my favorite quote by Louise Hay, the queen of self-healing, who pulled herself up from childhood sexual abuse and health issues and all kinds of traumas, wrote epic self-help books, and created a seminal publishing house in the 1980s. When it comes to role models in this healing space of people who turned pain and trauma into vast spiritual awakening and service to the collective, she is a great one to look to.

To show you how the concept of "feel it to heal it" works, I am going to share an example of how I lead one of my clients through my embodied transformational process and then guide you to work on one of your blocks, too.

When Kate came to me, she told me she wanted to feel confident, to be able to speak up, share her voice with the world, and be seen as her true self. But she thought people would think she was weird or "too much" if she shared. So she kept playing small, making her social media messages and pictures, her wardrobe, and her party persona super safe and likable. She would never share her real passions or opinions unless she was with close friends. And she just felt "not good enough" all the time, especially among other women.

Kate intuitively knew that as long as she was not claiming her authentic voice and heart, she would keep feeling shitty and dissatisfied with life. She would keep comparing herself to others and feeling generally unhappy in herself.

So first, I asked Kate to close here eyes and feel what she felt like when that *thing* came up. She told me she felt "small, weak, tight." From there, I asked her, "Okay what is the *thing*, the block, we are dealing with? Can you name it?" And she said, "Yes. It's my fear of being either too much or not good enough." Then I led her into her body, having her use breath and sound to get deeper into what that block felt like in her body. Turns out it was showing up mainly in her chest as anxiety and tightness. I had her magnify the feeling of anxiety and tightness through big, loud breaths and sounds, until tears were running down her cheeks.

Next, I asked her at what age she began to feel like this—too weird, too much, but also not good enough. She told me it had started when she was five and some kids at school said she was a weirdo because she liked to wear mismatched outfits. We acknowledged that a realization like this can sound so simple, silly even, and yet be enough to plague a person for years and years. And then I had her talk to that little girl inside who is still upset and let her have a *full moment* to express, to sing, to scream, to share herself with the world. I walked Kate into the depth of this wound, with sound and breath, asking her to feel the deepest part of the pain with me until she felt complete.

When the block didn't feel present in her chest anymore, it meant it was time to let the little girl part of Kate rest, so Kate the adult could stop struggling internally with this wound. "Are you ready to let go of this internal struggle between 'not good enough' and 'too much'?" I asked. Kate still had tears running down her face, but she was no longer *in* the wound. She had gotten to the other side. "Yes!" she told me. "I am so fucking ready to let go of this inner struggle!" I had her visualize holding the child part of herself, which doesn't happen in every session but felt good in this one.

With this separation, she could visualize that her child part was still driving her decisions from fear, and it was time to graduate from that so the current Kate could make decisions from love. We closed by using some slow, grounding breaths to bring Kate back into the room. With her eyes remaining closed, we felt into how the block in her chest was *now*, without the struggle. She told me it was gone. She felt freer—to dress how she wanted again, be a bit more wild, to stop worrying about what other people think all the time, and to come back to herself.

I left Kate with a simple universal tool: any time that old block came up, any time her wound was triggered, Kate would remind her little girl self: "I am the one in charge. I love you. I accept you. But I am running the show now." A simple internal reframe you can do when things feel sticky or painful as you begin to clean and rearrange the furniture of your internal world.

Your Turn

Pick one block, core wound, or internal narrative that is currently plaguing you or causing you pain or frustration. It doesn't have to be *huge*, but choose something substantial. Maybe it's a general anxiety or stress about something that happened or a limiting belief that is keeping you small.

1 **Feel it.** Breathe into your belly. Feel it in your body. Allow the thing to come forth, even though it may suck to feel it. Soften the belly. Soften the jaw. Soften the heart. Start with some deep belly breaths, your right hand on your lower belly, with your pinkie resting on your pubic bone. With each deep breath, feel the block or fear in you, in your body. If you feel numb or stuck, do *deeper,*

bigger belly breaths, accompanied by sighs. It will come. I promise. Hold the intention and the wound/block/belief in your heart as you breathe.

2 **Identify it.** Notice where this block is in your body. What color it is. What texture. What temperature. Notice if there is an image attached or a memory. Let it be present. Let it arise. Find it in your body, *not* by trying to analyze with your mind. Your mind will try to pull you into some stories and analysis, but just *breathe* whenever that happens. See the block. Let it be visual as it emerges in you and through you. Keep breathing.

3 **Magnify it.** Breathe into it more deeply and allow the feeling to get bigger. Sound it out with a "HA," moan it, scream it, cry it, allow the emotion to move through you however it needs to. You will feel as if you are drawing it forth, pulling it up and out, conjuring it from your depths. As if every cell is working with you to pull it up. If you can get on your hands and knees and that feels good, do that! If it moves through you like a gentle, or torrential, rain of tears, let them fall. If you feel anxiety below the surface like a crackling fire, breathe into *that*, free it, let your frustration and yearning *open* you.

4 **Let it move.** With breath, sound, and a visual, you can now allow whatever the block is to *move* through you and begin to transform. Allow the part of you that needs to be heard to come forth. See the wounded self or blocked self and let her speak. Let her scream, cry, and tell you what she needs. Listen until you feel complete.

5 **Release it.** Feel the shifts that may be happening within you. Is there a gift this wound or block has given you? Is there a way it can be turned into gold? Into a power instead of pain? Notice any insights, aha's, or breakthroughs. (Which may happen later, so no

need to force it.) Then visualize yourself. Notice how you feel, walk, talk, and carry yourself without that block, wound, or fear dominating you. Pull out your journal and take some notes.

If you want to do this guided by me, hop over to my website (alexandraroxo.com/flag) and download this practice. Thousands of people have done it and said it's life changing when they need to transform pain, or shame, or a piece of a wound, or a block. It's something you can do daily, from your phone, as your morning practice. Use it. It's free.

When you start to become aware of your core issues, they may rise up and be mirrored more blatantly in your life. At times, it can feel scary and frustrating as they manifest before your eyes to be healed. This is an opportunity to transform them. It takes strength, practice, and clarity, and that's why I've outlined ways to support yourself through this healing process. Your life becomes your art, as you see each moment as an opportunity to transform and be reborn through facing the shadows you call to the light.

Soon enough it'll become second nature, and you'll be able to do it anytime a block pops up, but it will help to have me guide you as you get started into this process of healing yourself. Because *yes*—you now have a simple embodied way to begin to heal your wounds and transform them into your gifts. *Fuck yeah.* This is a way to use any tough and tricky feelings as tools for your awakening, instead of running from them or shoving them back down inside. You have already reclaimed so much power by simply facing the tough shit. By acknowledging what needs work. By being vulnerable with yourself and by honoring your story. Your pain. And your glory. By you opening those closets and airing them out, cleaning them out, you are finding space for more joy, more love, more peace. You may feel taller. Clearer. Stronger. You just need *you*, your breath, your body, your voice, an open heart, and courage. And you have all that.

HOW TO RECLAIM
YOUR SEXUAL POWER

A woman unafraid of her shadows radiates light.
The fact that she has accepted her darkest parts,
The most embarrassing, the most shameful,
The things society says are weird or gross or unacceptable—
The fact that she has turned those things into her allies gives her
   immense power.

She shines when she walks into a room.
She has nothing to be afraid of.
She doesn't need you to like her or approve of her.
She doesn't need to be validated.

She's just there being an imperfect woman, fierce, loving,
And standing tall in every moment of her celebrated imperfections.

She doesn't need to put on a facade pretending she's okay all the time.
She isn't okay. Or not okay. She just *is*.

She's been to the depths of her own hells and back again.
She keeps facing the fears and becoming more and more present,
   radiant, strong.

She is *you*.

AS YOU MAY already be discovering, the more that we get to know ourselves and the more aware we become of our own baggage, the more it creeps up! Not just to be creepy, but so you can further accept and integrate it and allow it to transform into a gift. This is *true* healing, and it is miraculously beautiful. Many people think that taking the spiritual or healing path means becoming more peaceful, more conscious about their food choices, maybe doing a daily affirmation, some yoga. And *yes*, all of that can be a part of the path. But all of these external practices can be tools to help us become more conscious of the internal wounds and caverns and gnarled bits that need tending to. The pain, the wounds, and the conditioning that live deep in our shadows are waiting to be called into the light, loved, sat with, held, and invited home.

And for myself, the collective, and most of us, sex is an area where the shadows run deep.

Again, here's how I often see this playing out:

- You are born beautiful and whole, a being of pure love, as I mentioned before.

- At some point in your childhood, you learn about what sex simply is. You become innocently curious. You explore. You play. And likely you reach a point where some shame comes in. (An example: Mom caught you masturbating at age five and told you that you were a bad little girl. You felt ashamed of certain aspects of your sexuality, pushing them into your shadow.) Or you may reject a part of your sexuality or your sexual desires because of family, societal, or religious conditioning, or you experienced sexual trauma, and therefore bits of your true sexual essence get shoved in the shadows.

- As an adult, you learn most people in Western society don't talk much about sex openly. As many countries were colonized by the values of the British Puritans, in many ways those values still hold true, and real sex is still taboo. For example: you can have whatever sex you want, but you may feel too shy or vulnerable to speak about deep or nuanced sexual topics—like, say, the quality of your orgasms, or if you partner is retaining his semen or expelling it and why, or how sexual union can be a completely transcendental experience— so your sexual self stays below the surface, hidden and repressed. Another example of sexuality gone into shadow: your pleasure gets put on the back burner of your busy work life, and the exploration of your sexuality and pleasure becomes buried in the shadows under your ambition.

There are many ways sex can be a wound, or a place of shadow for us. We are sexual beings by nature, so if we don't tend to that part of ourselves, it will come find us in surprising, weird, and frustrating ways. You may find yourself being judgmental toward other people's sexuality. You may feel a sense of shame that can't be pinned on something specific. As our buddy Carl Jung mentioned, that hidden shadow part will pop up and say, "*Boo!*" when we least expect it. You may also feel blocks in your physical body around your sexuality: being unable to orgasm with a partner (like me when

I was younger), for example. You may be tight in the hips. Get stuck in your head during sex. You may get feelings of nausea or the heebie-jeebies watching sexual scenes on TV or in movies. If one of your partners tries to get dirty with you, your reaction may be to say, "Hell, no!!" and break up with them! Your shadow comes back to haunt you, stealing your joy and cramping your full radiant power.

So how do you stop this cycle?

Well, as we are learning, you stop and you face the motherfucking thing! As I shared in the last chapter, the only way to overcome our most shadowy fears is to look them straight in the eye, dance with them, breathe them, feel them, allow them to transform, and welcome them *home*.

Many spiritual traditions and cultures have practices of facing our shadows and embodying them so we can either release them and integrate them or simply give them a space to play. Halloween, for example, is symbolic of this: dressing up as goblins, demons, and monsters is a way to give our shadows a place to dance. Unfortunately, the sacredness of this rite has been lost, and little kids today have no effing clue why they're dressing like a vampire! How cool would it be if our moms had been, like, "Honey. You know that part of you that screams, 'I want a new mommy' every time I try to get you in the bath? Well, tonight you get to dress as your inner vampire shadow demon child so you can get it all out!"

The fact that so many women dress "sexy" for Halloween is a *big* clue about how many of us are harboring shadows about our sexuality, because of religion, the patriarchy, inherited beliefs in our families—and also sexual trauma. A big part of my work has been creating safe spaces for women to share their stories and feel the unprocessed feelings of their sexual traumas and shame, and I've learned that most women on this planet—as well as many nonbinary and trans people, and men too—have experienced some form of sexual trauma or abuse, big or small, in their lives.

When it comes to sex, the shadows holding these traumas can trip us like a pair of heels you forgot you left on the bedroom floor, leaving us embarrassed at best, if not hurting and even afraid.

We are going to be courageous and talk about all the things about sex that we have been afraid of, that we wished we could have discussed with our parents or friends. In doing so we'll release the blocks that are keeping us feeling tight, and small, and harboring shame deep below the surface. Here's how it happened for me.

How Ashamed I Was of My Sexuality and How I Broke Free

The shadow of sexual shame found me at an early age. My childhood conditioning left me so deeply ashamed for being me and for being a sexual being that it took me until my thirties to fully undo that shame and be free of it.

Growing up in Georgia in a Protestant Bible-belt world sent me the message early on: "Sexuality is *bad*. You are a sinner." But spending summers in Brazil with my dad, I got the opposite message: "Your sexuality is your currency as a woman. You had better be sexy, well kempt, and ready to entertain the men around you." Two contradictory messages that shaped my relationship to sex and being a woman. In Georgia, I remember being told masturbation was sinful. I remember being told women's bodies were to be hidden and not to be shared until marriage. I learned that if I explored sexually as a young girl in this Christian Bible-belt world, I would be risking my friends and my reputation, and I would likely go to hell! But my innate desire to be a young woman feeling wild and free in her body was bigger than my fear of what would happen if I did. So I started asking questions about sexuality.

And I started being called a slut. A whore. I was twelve years old! I hadn't even had sex. I hadn't so much as given a blow job. I simply was unafraid of expressing my sensual side in the way I walked and talked and dressed, and I wasn't afraid to be curious.

Hanging with my cousins in the summers in Brazil, they would laugh at my Land's End one-piece swimsuit and pull out a string bikini for me that barely covered my tiny nipples. They would teach me how to dance samba and grind my hips over the mouth of a bottle in a dance that was the rage at the time. And the adults encouraged it! They weren't encouraging us to literally have sex, but they liked the young women to dance wildly, to wear revealing clothes, and to get our hair and nails done. In one way, the Brazilians were celebrating women's sexuality, through dance, song, food, freedom—and I will forever be grateful for this counterbalance to my Bible-belt conditioning in Georgia.

But I also remember watching TV at my dad's house when I was about six or seven years old. I was bored and looking through the VHS tapes for something new to watch. I found a tape and held it up. It had a cartoon on the front of a naked woman and a donkey—yes, it was porn! My dad screamed at me: "Did you watch this video?!" Even though I said no (I hadn't), he made me go and cry in my room in the dark for hours, shame around sex brewing through my tiny veins. His shame, which probably came from his parents, and from their parents, now passed down to me. This is how most wounds gets inherited.

I remember once hearing my dad having sex with a girlfriend when I was about twelve and feeling like I was going to vomit. I suppose in some day and age this would be deemed normal and healthy—adults having sex, sounds being heard. But for me, because sex had been shrouded by shame and guilt, to be forced to listen to it brought me great pain and confusion. I finally couldn't let the shame brew under my skin anymore. So I went into the kitchen and took a glass out of the cabinet and threw it at the floor with all my might, as if shattering the glass would shatter my own pain, shame, and confusion. I also hoped it would jar them out of their own unconscious behavior, not taking into consideration that a small girl could hear it all. They kept going. I broke three glasses that day. And I swept them up. No one ever heard or knew. But the pain and confusion I felt had to leave my body somehow. That was the only way I knew to express it then.

Sex confused me. It upset me. And I was also deeply intrigued by it. If the conditioning of the Catholic church on my dad's side wasn't enough, adding to it the Bible-belt conservatism, the Brazilian sexiness, and the paradoxical nature of it all helped to further instill in me the feeling that sex was something contradictory and problematic for most humans and most religions. Feared! Kept behind closed doors. Not spoken about, with truth and an open heart.

So you can see how we begin to develop the shadow of sexual shame, or guilt, or confusion, often pushing this part of us into the background, to be taken out only in dark, locked rooms and discussed over copious amounts of wine or in therapy.

And the moments of shame likely don't just happen in childhood. We continue to get mixed messages around sex from the media, spirituality, religion, social norms. When I was thirty-one, I remember the sexual shame shadow creeping over me like a hundred-pound lead blanket when my best friend said she couldn't sleep in my room because she "didn't want to sleep on my jizz-stained sheets"—I had been sleeping with a man at the time and having amazing sex. Her words pierced me and hit my wound of sexual shame like a dart to a bull's-eye. Again, what I heard was that being a sexual woman was *still* something to be ashamed of and that me being free, feeling empowered to do what felt right for me at the time, was something to be ashamed of.

Another reason sex is such a touchy and tender subject is because so many of us have experienced sexual assault. I believe that sexuality being suppressed by religion has led to rape and sexual abuse being used as weapons of power and control and that the shadow of the repression of the feminine principle, or the fear of "the Other," has been externalized as sexual abuse, rape, and molestation. Rape is often a weapon in war. Rape has been a weapon of slavery and a weapon used in conjunction with the genocide and colonization of indigenous peoples. It's a weapon statistically used mainly against women, children, and people of color (including indigenous peoples), or whomever the patriarchy silently defines as the weaker or inferior parties on this planet.

Now it is on us to speak up and say: "This is *not* okay!" All of us. And of course this battle cry is happening and has been for some time, though collectively the dominant culture has only recently begun to start processing the atrocities it has committed.

In order to make these shifts as a collective, I believe we need to face our individual sexual shadow first. I'm going to tell you how I did it—and also share the sexual trauma I have experienced and moved through in this life, finding joy and pleasure in my body again after it, and letting the experiences empower me to take a stand, claim my power, and share my voice with the world.

The first sexual assault I experienced was a date rape at age twenty. I was in Prague visiting some friends on my fall break from NYU and went out to a local bar. I remember making eyes with a Czech man whom my friends knew. There was an electricity between us. I was tipsy, and I went home with him. My American friends didn't intervene, even though I had no cell phone and my passport was at my friend's house, on some street I didn't have the name of. I walked down the dark streets of Prague with him, thinking, "I don't know where I am. I don't know this city. I don't know how to get back to my friends." In that moment I woke up to the fact I should *not* have left the bar with this man. I went into survival mode, and my body released adrenaline, and a whole hormonal cocktail of fear sobered me up from the few Czech beers I had drunk.

When we arrived at his college dorm room, his behavior switched from kindness to aggression: he pulled my clothes off, bent me over a desk, and forced himself on me. I remember the feeling of leaving my body and watching myself from the ceiling, like a floating angel or a cloud drifting by. I completely dissociated from the experience, my awareness finding my body again only in brief moments, like when he changed his position.

Afterward, I was pulled back into my body by a tear hitting my chest. My tear. As if it weighed a thousand pounds, it fell on me and jarred me back into the visceral experience I had dissociated from. I thought, "Holy shit. Did this really happen?" I had no idea how to get home, so I was forced to stay the night. In the morning I played nice and asked him to call my friends, smiling a plastic smile, knowing that he could throw me out on the street and I would have no passport or way home. I was in survival mode. A mode you know all too well if you've been through trauma or terror. His friend came over, and he ripped my shirt off in front of him. I prayed fervently until he took me back to my friends. When, eventually, I was reunited with them, I didn't know how to explain what had happened. Instead I left the Czech Republic and traveled on to

Spain alone. I remember lying in the fetal position in a tiny room in Seville in shock. Eventually I made a lot of art about that experience as a part of my healing.

Throughout my twenties I experienced multiple other attempted assaults, by both men and women. Waking up with a man on top of me while staying at a friend's place. A woman pinning me down at another friend's house one summer, so drunk she passed out on top of me and I couldn't get out from under her. I've also been chased down streets. Stalked. Grabbed.

I used to wonder why. Bad karma? Like many people who have been through an assault, part of me wondered if it was my fault. (PSA: It is *never* our fault.) I realized that walking through the world as a sexually free and open and empowered woman could be risky. And I learned that in order to do it I needed to be warrior-like at times, have a strong daily practice and a real sense of myself, take care with drugs and alcohol, embrace a rad community, find strong support, and have faith in something bigger than me. Because, no, I am not going to play small or stay small because the world can't handle it. Nope. It's a scary subconscious thing we often do, this staying small. It doesn't mean we should blast our energy all over the place carelessly, but we must allow ourselves to emerge into life fully. It makes sense that we have played small in order to keep ourselves safe, but I have learned there are other ways to create a sense of safety and find balance.

So I have had to tell myself: It's okay to be sexual. It's okay to be powerful. It's okay to be free. It's okay to be *exactly* who you are. And it's important you have strong self-care and amazing boundaries in order to be this revolutionary and expressed in the world.

My experiences, as a child and as a grown woman, left a deep imprint of sexual shame in me until I faced them. And now, if shame arises (which it rarely does), I know to look at it instead of push it away—so that I can make a choice to accept myself, no matter what the world has taught me about what it means to be a sexual woman.

Shame will suck away your power and beauty if you let it. But, ultimately, it is a gateway into parts of yourself that hold massive power. So let's make friends with shame and look into our shadows, until there is no longer anything to be afraid of.

Turn Sexual Shame into Your Teacher and Guide

Once I was riding in a car back from Joshua Tree with a few progressive people whom I love. It was a long car ride, and the conversation turned to sex. A friend mentioned that the man she was dating loved blow jobs. Then I said something about having a mind-blowing orgasm when a yogi filmmaker and I were engaging in conscious kink, playing with pain, and that I was in an altered state of bliss for three days after. The car went quiet. What did I say? Was it the trance of bliss or... the kink? It was consensual, of course, but I had crossed some sort of invisible line. I wondered: "How come blow jobs are okay to discuss, but a spanking is too hardcore for conscious folks? Couldn't conscious spanking exist? And where is safe to talk about real sex if not with people we love?" Most of all, I felt ashamed of my "freaky" sexual tendencies, and I internalized this and stopped speaking. It was clear that discussing some of my sexual adventures, even among the most progressive circles, could be seen as "too much." Did someone in the car experience an encounter similar to mine that didn't result in arousal? It's possible. Was it the wrong space to chat about sex openly? Possibly. But if so, where is the right one?

Anytime we open the doors to talk about sex, there is a possibility that shame or pain will arise, as we are dealing with a vault of human experience that has been repressed for millennia, resulting in mass pain and trauma. But does that mean we keep hiding it away? No. In order to heal, we must actually start talking about it—the good, the bad, and the ugly—in safe places and with people we trust. In sacred spaces. With love and understanding and intentionality and no judgment.

Sexual shame can prevent us from living a healthy sex life, first and foremost, which is one reason to face it. But we often bring it to other areas of life, too! Our repressed sexual shame can show up in friendships, as jabs at friends who may trigger something in us. It can show up as menstrual cramps, IBS, self-confidence issues. Sexual shame is often an elephant in the room in today's world.

Here again, as with every part of the transformational process, change begins with awareness.

To be able to hold space for awareness around sexual shame, you must first create a safe space internally. Acknowledging your sexual shame and coming to your own internal acceptance about anything that may have instilled this in you is the place to start. From here, we can begin to process emotions that are stored away relating to your sexuality—emotions that are preventing you from fucking like a goddess.

As we move through the transformational work in this chapter, your core wounds may come up, reflected in your daily life, relationships, and thoughts. You may attract some situations that trigger your wounding and may serve as opportunities for healing. Remember, this is how you know it's working! This is not a bad thing. This is productive. It's really important to let yourself feel whatever surfaces and not be afraid. Each emotion, each trigger, and each memory that arises is important. Do what you need to do to be safe, take it at whatever pace you need, care for yourself.

If you have had many sexual experiences that were intrusive and nonconsensual or are holding on to a lot of sexual shame, this may feel like a no-go zone for you. That is okay. I trust you to trust yourself and tread with gentleness and care. If perhaps this book is pointing you in the direction of seeking one-on-one work with a trusted counselor, that is amazing too. I trust you also to know when to stop if something feels like it's too much for your system. When to take a pause and breathe. And when to keep going into the work. This takes a lot of awareness and discernment, skills you will cultivate over time, in your daily practice and contemplative work.

For me, dealing with multiple sexual assaults and healing through the resultant pain in my system has happened in steps over the years. In circles. In writing. Journaling. Feeling. Therapy. With coaches. In ceremonies. And most of that I did on a very limited budget; somehow I called it in. It's definitely been a 360 approach, and I didn't have a road map. I went with my gut. So go with yours. Feel into what is right for you.

Keep up with your daily practice. Take impeccable care of yourself. Ask a friend for support. Take an Epsom salts bath; salt is clearing for the system, and a bath can detoxify you, clear your energy, and help you feel held. (Consult the Internet for many recipes and scientific data about this.) Other ways to move energy that feels sticky in your body: have a deep cry, punch a pillow, find a place to have a good scream, shake your body out or dance vigorously, write like you're vomiting words in your journal, go to a steam room or sauna. Whatever you do, letting the feelings move out of your body is key. And, again, do not be afraid of the depth and breadth of the feelings that may come up when you are doing this work. Instead, look at it as an opportunity to reclaim some of your power. Remember that before acceptance may come rage, sadness, anger, and fear, and all of this is *okay*.

If you've already been doing the exercises and practices in this book, you will know by now that emotions come and go like waves. That they don't define you.

Okay. Let's do this.

THE TRANSFORMATIONAL WORK: GET REAL ABOUT YOUR SEXUAL PAST

This topic is vast, complex, ugly, delicious, exciting, scary, and real. It encompasses a lot of collective wounding that may hold treasures for our awakening process. It is central to the work of this book, so stay with me. Take a breath. As discussed, read this in a safe space and cozy up with yourself. Light a candle. Shut the door.

Sexual Inventory Ritual: Part 1

First of all, let's look at some beliefs about sex that may be present. Open your journal and ask yourself:

- What is my current relationship to sex?
- What beliefs around sex did I grow up with?
- What stories do I keep telling myself around sex?
- What did my parents teach me about sex when I was growing up?

This is you taking inventory to *get real about where you are at*. Remember: as with everything I will ask of you here, there is no right or wrong answer. Whatever your personal history includes is true for you. So don't be afraid.

Now, I want you to think about little you. How did that sweet you experience first hearing about sex? First feeling sexual? What were the first ways you experimented with these exciting feelings?

Breathe. This may be intense to open up to. But in order to reclaim your full sexual power, you will need to look at where you are repressing it, suppressing it, or even disavowing it completely. We will dive deeper into this work together in the next chapter. I guarantee that as you look at it, integrate it, claim it, love it, and in doing so tend to its most broken and wounded parts, you will feel bigger, taller, stronger, and sexier. You will begin to feel *invincible*.

Sexual Inventory Ritual: Part 2

I mentioned how when I was twenty-two I was ready to have my first orgasm with a partner. This exercise is what got me there. I can't say that it will have that impact across the board. But what it did for me was bring greater awareness to all my sexual experiences, allowing me to open all the closets and let the skeletons loose so I could clean house.

This ritual is not about saying, "Forgive me my sins!" It is just about accepting ourselves and our pasts and allowing any insights to emerge as we review our experiences from a new perspective. This act of self-review and self-acceptance around sex may sound simplistic, but as you sit with the experiences that come up, notice any hidden guilt, shame, disgust, and anger that arise. We are going to examine these feelings and in doing so transmute any repressed shadow parts into exalted spaces of love and power.

If you have experienced any level of sexual trauma, or if you know this may be a tough one for you, please do this exercise gently. Perhaps do it with a friend, have a coach supervise, or if you have a therapist, let them know you're going to do it. Take full responsibility for your healing process and well-being, knowing that unearthing these memories may trigger you into sadness, anxiety, or depression. Spread this work out over the week, perhaps going an hour at a time, then taking a break so you don't get lost in the depths. It will work just the same.

1 **Set your sacred space.** Turn your phone on airplane mode. Put on some gentle music if it suits you. Give yourself an allotted amount of time and close and lock your doors.

2 **Make a nest.** Whether it's on the living room floor or on your bed, I love to create a cozy space for myself with my favorite blankets and pillows when I am going to do deep work like this.

3 **Grab your journal, pen, and some tissues just in case.**

4 **Start by belly breathing.** Breathe deeply into your belly as you do the work. Let your belly relax and be soft. The more deeply you allow yourself to relax, the more you will be able to drop into the tender, shadowy parts of yourself. Notice those moments when you clamp down and start to come out of the breath.

5 **When you're ready, you can begin writing.** Start to take inventory of your first sexual experiences and how they felt to you. Write a few sentences minimum for each one—and if you feel like writing two or three pages, go for it! Stay connected to your breath, which will bring this practice into the body, where the healing is. If emotions arise, do not swallow them down. If you feel grief, cry. If you feel rage, scream. If you feel excitement, laugh! There are many ways to express feelings so they can move rather than get stuck. After allowing an emotion to come up and move through you, see if you can come back to neutral by breathing deeply. If you are a meditator, you may know this space of returning to neutral as the space of being a "witness," watching the mind but not engaging in its drama. As you practice this skill, you may find you can stay in a witness state for only a short time

before the mind pulls you back into the muck of all the crazy feelings and internal drama. But with dedicated practice and daily meditation, you will learn to hop back into a neutral space of being present. As I always say: the breath is the bridge. From the past to the present. From the drama to peace. Stay in the deep breathing. Just breathe. This is the most important part. Without the breath and depth, this is simply a writing exercise.

6 **When your timer goes off, close the journal.** *Do not* reread what you wrote. Let it be.

7 **Close the ritual.** You can do this by dancing to a song to shake some energy out of your body, or by doing some deep breathing. You can burn some incense or take a salt bath and then move on to the next part of your day. It's very important you create an ending so you don't get stuck in any lingering memories or feelings. You have agency to say: "I am done now."

8 **Repeat this ritual daily until you have made it through your whole sexual inventory.**

This exercise may take one hour a day for a week, or it could be done in one sitting! There's no "correct" pace at which to move—it's up to you to pace it.

Now that you have a clearer view and the internal closets are getting aired out, you may find yourself in barre class thinking about that one partner who did that thing that pissed you off or turned you on. You may get annoyed, angry, sad, frustrated, excited—all from that one memory, all in the space of a forty-five-minute class! This is when you have got to call on your own inner protector goddess to come in and calm you, reminding you to return to the present moment. When you find yourself getting off on an old memory or becoming enraged by it, you can move that energy with free movement or dance or with one of my recorded guided practices. If you're at work or in the car, then talk directly to the part of you that is obsessing over, grasping at, and replaying that scene: "Hi, love! We are leaving all that *in the ritual space*. Here, in this moment, we are going to be present. We are going to do our work in the container we created for the work and not outside of it. Thank you!" And if you feel called to reach out to someone from your past, I ask you to wait. To breathe. First, to write a letter that you do not send. And sit on that for a bit. You can flush it, burn it, or bury it. Wait some more. And if the urge to contact the person is still super present, speak with a trusted friend, coach, or guide to help you assess if that's the best action for you to take or if perhaps there's more unraveling and healing to be done within yourself first.

Sexual Inventory Ritual: Part 3

Set your sacred space again, but this time bring in a mirror. And put on some *epic* tunes. (I have many great playlists in my public Spotify to support deep internal work.) Go back to the pages of your journal from the previous exercise and follow the steps below.

1   Going through each name on your list one at a time, look at yourself in the mirror and say: "If I am still holding any shame, guilt, disgust, or pain about the experience I had with this person, then what is it here to teach me? Am I ready to accept this experience with love and compassion for myself?" If it's a yes, then while gazing into your own eyes in the mirror, say "Thank you" to the person for helping you to wake up, for being your teacher, and then commit to letting the person go. (By "letting go" I mean no longer harping on them, speaking of them, or complaining about the experience you had with them.)

If there is still a lot of energy there, and you don't feel quite ripe for "thank you," feel free to say "Fuck you" to them in the mirror and keep working on it. Be aware that you are still working through the lessons that person or situation *brought* you, that it is no longer about them, and that that is okay. If you feel complete with the lesson, you can end by saying: "I am willing to feel any emotions that are creating a link between myself and this person or experience, so that I may set this person free from my consciousness and move on."

Repeat this process with all or as many experiences as you need to complete. Notice how you feel as you do it. *See* yourself in the mirror. You can amend the words to fit what feels right for you. You either have more work to do with the lesson (not necessarily the person) or you feel complete with the lesson. Don't judge yourself. Accepting where you are is part of the medicine of this work.

2 Tear the pages into tiny pieces and burn, bury, or flush them. If you want to burn them, you can do this in a fireplace if you have access to one, but you can just as easily light a little scrap of paper, let it burn, and then drop it into a pot of water on the stove. At the end, take the pot and pour the remnants down the toilet with a nice, big flush. (Carefully curate the song that will be your soundtrack for this part of the ritual!) Afterward, burn incense, take a salt bath, or have a dance party to move that energy through and out of your body. Burying or flushing the paper works well also.

3 Now feel into the space you have regained internally. This may emerge in time; it's not always an instant thing. The most painful experiences may take more time to accept and integrate, and that is okay.

You have done some really deep work here. I know it's not easy. It takes a lot of courage to open those closets and dig out the old, musty bits *and* the buried treasures. But now it's done. Please do a victory dance. Laugh loudly. Have a delightful bath. Do some breath work. Don't hang on to whatever came up. Shake it out. Breathe it out. You've just made peace with some deep parts of you. You've made more space in your heart because you are carrying around less shit. Imagine what magic may come into your life now that you're not running the sexual shame app under all the other stuff. You're free to write a new story now. Your own. And that is magical.

HOW TO COME HOME
TO YOUR BODY

To be in this body means to be nature.
To live as nature.
I surrender to this process.
I surrender to being like a seed that flowers and grows and
    wilts and is reborn.
I am cyclical, like the seasons.
Like the moon, which wanes from shining in full light
To "Look at me" (I am invisible, I am gone, I am darkness,
    I am going void).

'Tis a strange way to be, to be a circle like this—a cycle
Of one moment shine and the next moment dark.
But this is me, in a body, everyday surrender, ups and downs,
    and I am willing.

It requires courage to be in this body,
Like jumping into a river and simply letting it carry you
But keeping your head above the water so you can see
    not to bang into a rock.

It would seem easier to be a static point!
Or a line, fixed, unchanging, known,
Finite, transparent. Than the circle spiral.

But this process of being in this body is mine.
I am going to claim it.

YOUR BODY IS YOUR TRUE HOME for this lifetime. It houses your glorious heart, your mind, and your spirit. It is the physicalized *you*. The externalized *you*. Chances are it is also the part of you that has received the most stress, trauma, and programming (from parents, religion, and media) and possibly the most pain.

So much of emotional and spiritual healing focuses on the mind and psyche, and often the body is overlooked as the seat of potential transformation. But the body is *essential* to our healing and transformational process. In his book *The Body Keeps the Score*, psychiatrist and trauma expert Bessel van der Kolk reminds us that "imprints from the past can be transformed by having physical experiences that directly contradict the helplessness, rage, and collapse that are part of trauma, and thereby regaining self-mastery." In my embodied healing program, my mentees and I spent a weekend with master Japanese rope bondage practitioner Victoria "Blue" of VoxBody Studio in Oakland, California, having our bodies tied and suspended in ropes. The act of being deeply constricted as a *choice* was incredibly healing for the body, creating a womblike sense of surrender and of being held. One of the women in my program, Columbia University–trained sex therapist Allie Lerner, shared that: "The experience of being consensually bound/tied up/constricted/controlled healed my sexual trauma in more significant ways than any other intervention I've tried, including therapy."

As a healer and practitioner, finding ways for myself and other women to heal *in* the body has been a key part of my work. Throughout time, religion, myth, and media, the female body has often been made to seem dirty, sinful, and open for scrutiny. It has been covered, coveted, constricted, and controlled. From approximately 17.5 million voluntary cosmetic surgeries performed in the US in 2017 (according to the American Society of Plastic Surgeons) to $39 billion spent the same year on lingerie worldwide (per Zion Market Research), manipulating, changing, and packaging the female body is a multi-billion-dollar industry. Every day, hundreds of ads send us the message "You'll be lovable if you have shiny hair! Buy this!" or "You'll be more popular with big breasts! Buy this!" No wonder so many women have suffered from disordered eating and body dysmorphia. It is not always easy trying to fit the mold of how physical beauty has been defined for us by society.

On a deeper level, the female body has long been subjected to religious control and the pain of war. This often also ties into the global collective sexual narrative and shadow. According to UNICEF, at least 200 million girls and women alive today in thirty countries have undergone female genital mutilation. And according to the International Labour Organization, 4.8 million people are currently trapped in forced sexual exploitation globally. These numbers alert us that core aspects of the cultural and ancestral pain and shadow of our centuries-old oppression are coursing through our collective DNA right here and now.

It is completely necessary that we grieve, we rage, we mourn, we scream, we cry about *all of this*. We've often been directly and indirectly told to focus on the mind, to concentrate on personal ambition and materialism, and to *avoid* looking at the greater global issues we participate in if we are operating within the systems of the countries holding the global financial power. It is up to us to express our feelings about global injustices and scream, share, rage, and ultimately find the courage to create change however we can. *It starts with us.* In our bodies. If we are *free* to speak, to cry, to come home to our own bodies and heal, then we must fall to our knees and say, "*Thank you* that we have this ability!" We must do it for those who cannot. We must take the internalized self-hate we gobbled down from a broken system and turn it into power, to make change in the world.

It all starts in the *body*. The hands. The heart. The voice. The sex organs. We reclaim *all of it*.

You may be wondering, "But what if I've been hating my body my whole life? Taught I am worthless?" Doing a 180 and deciding to love the body you are in may not be easy. It has taken me years of work. But I am here to tell you it is possible. And *essential* to our collective healing.

If you've struggled with body image issues, disordered eating, body shaming, body dysmorphia, and/or orthorexia (coined in 1998 as "an obsession with healthy eating"), the fallout doesn't just go away overnight. And if you have not had this personal struggle or karmic curriculum, perhaps you know someone who has. If you yourself have faced or currently face this struggle, perhaps there are times when your body feels ugly, painful, or disturbing. In the grip of body hatred, it can feel like there's a voice soundtracking every moment of your day, telling you, "You're gross" or some other kind of self-judgment or critique. And that little voice can ruin everything: every potential idea, every instance when you could speak up, moments of connection, and moments of love. It sabotages your power and your life-force. The voice of inner criticism can shrink you down to the size of a pea, silencing the brilliance in you and distracting you from the *joy* that is available to you in each and every moment—if only you are able to see it.

Imagine if, when kids were told in school about the changes that would happen in their bodies, they were taught to embrace them? For cisgendered females, perhaps there would be a guidebook: "Okay, so once a month you may feel really out of sorts. You may get bloated. But you may also have a magical capacity to sense your intuition! Your heart may be more sensitive. You may be attuned to the divine energies in you, and you may find yourself feeling in tune with nature. Don't wear tight clothes at this time; it'll make it worse. Drink lots of water. Eat chocolate and root veggies. Take baths. It's okay to cry, a lot if you need to. Find the beauty in alone time that week, tune in to yourself, and listen to your inner voice."

I wish someone had told me all this. But having to find my own way has allowed me to write my own narratives around my body and my menstrual cycle, identify and erase the collective conditioning, and ultimately find myself in a land that feels like truth.

Whether political, social, cultural, or personal, the stories of the past are written all over our bodies. But now is when we get to rewrite the script.

My Body, My Power Source

As with everything, seeing our parents' relationship to their bodies, to food, and to sex is how we developed our own behaviors and beliefs in these areas. Both my parents had complex relationships with all these things.

My father started talking about my body size when I was pretty young. He would say to me: "You must be careful, or you'll get fat." In my still-forming preteen mind, this imprinted as: "You are not lovable by dad [that is, *men*] if you're not thin." The wider message—supported by everything I saw in the media—was that "humans are not lovable when fat." Over and over and over, I internalized the belief that my worthiness and lovability were contingent on my weight.

That is a tough one to undo, and it's a shadow belief that takes up a *lot* of mental and emotional space for many humans. If we had healthy relationships to food, exercise, and our bodies, imagine how much energy we'd have for climate change solutions, innovations to provide food and housing for those in need, creative visions that welcome in a new golden age of art and culture, and embracing and prioritizing play? What might our world be like if we hadn't been imprinted with cultural narratives around thinness, if we hadn't been sold on processed foods, like soda and sugar, and if feeding one's body with healthy, whole foods available to all socioeconomic groups was a part of the collective narrative?

In my own journey, I was labeled young as a "smart girl" and was a classic overachiever, and so I set my my ambitions high; but I also bought into the collective narrative I had yet to examine, that I must be beautiful and thin to be of value in this world. This created an ongoing internal struggle. I learned I needed resources that my mom and I didn't have in order to follow this cultural narrative: money to go to exercise classes, to get my nails and hair done, to buy clothes and shoes, et cetera. I quickly recognized that looking good as per society's standards was a position of privilege.

My attempts to follow the collective unspoken rules of beauty and body conflicted with my attempts to contribute to the world for the betterment of all beings—volunteering at homeless shelters, writing plays, mentoring teens in theater, and pursuing my own ambitions. I ended up with a vast internal gap that took decades for me to bridge.

It was around age twelve that I started counting calories, taking laxatives, and going to the gym. Though I didn't know it at the time, I was clearly looking for love, acceptance, and a sense of belonging. I was an only child. My mom worked full time in a city more than an hour away. My dad didn't live close to me. We spoke on the phone for a few minutes a week. It wasn't logical that me being thin would bring his love back into my life or give me a sense of belonging, but the subconscious stories dictated my conscious life, and my fight with my body began.

For the next nineteen years or so, the quiet, socially acceptable, insidious shadow of body shame and control would come in and out of my life. And I wasn't the only one. So many girls and women I knew were also watching what they ate, working out constantly, and taking diet pills and laxatives that these things felt normal. We were all looking for something we didn't have words for.

Most young Western girls don't have designated rites of passage, or rituals, or places to feel all the complex feelings occurring as we transition into womanhood. Perhaps we don't know how to manage the feelings, so we may stop eating as a way to try to numb and control them, the hunger and obsession about food taking up so much space that there is no space to experience the beautiful, albeit weird, transition into being a woman. When I was a teen in Marietta, Georgia, most of my friends had stopped eating in a way that was healthy. A few were exercising like maniacs. Some were cutting themselves. And many were drinking a lot. Living in a capitalist, materialist society that lacked a common spiritual thread, tools for self-healing, a sense of community and togetherness, a connection to the earth, or mentorship from elders impacted us all.

I remember my friend Sarah showing me the cuts on her inner wrists during PE class when we were fifteen, and I almost vomited. Her father had left, and she had no tools for coping with her pain. I was counting calories and taking laxatives, she was cutting, and we didn't ever speak about *why* we were hurting ourselves, nor did we know how or where to ask for help.

We also had *power* and creativity and sexuality we were not expressing, so we used alcohol, pain, laxatives, et cetera to dumb down the pain in us—and the *divine* trying to come out through us. The voices. The stories. The *truths* we had buried in our hearts. But our tiny high schools and sterile churches and empty shopping malls had no spaces for us and our *big magic*. So we pushed it down.

The nights I spent lying on the bathroom floor in agony were partly a way to distract myself from feeling a lack of belonging and a longing for a different world, a sense of home, wholeness, and freedom. But they were also a way for me to actually feel the *pain* in my heart. They were a way of purging my pain.

I was never bulimic or anorexic to the point of needing hospitalization or treatment, but my disordered eating gnawed at my soul throughout high school. It dimmed during my early twenties when I began making art as a way to express my confusion and pain at being in this world and no longer felt the need to control my eating and exercise habits. But then it returned with a vengeance when I was twenty-seven and my girlfriend of two years, whom I thought was the love of my life, cheated on me. My childhood wound of abandonment from my father opened, I fell into what felt like an infinite abyss of pain, and I stopped eating.

As a relatively privileged white woman in a world full of intractable problems, I eventually took full responsibility to work through the guilt about the self-inflicted pain I had put my body through over the years. After much self-inquiry, healing, meditation, and transformation, I realized I could have been doing so much else with my life-force energy had I had the tools to begin healing earlier on my path. But the pain of losing myself, of losing love, of losing a parent, of being sexually abused, of being abandoned—these pains had nowhere else to live, it seemed, no circles of women to cry in at the time, no rituals to heal with, and they had to come out through my body somehow. And I'm not alone in having gone through this battle. This is a tragedy that impacts humans by the millions. Recent studies conclude that more than 30 million people of all ages and genders suffer from eating disorders in the US alone. There are varying degrees of this struggle. If along your journey you feel like you need outside care or assistance for your particular path, please seek a professional in the field, such as a therapist.

I came out on the other side of my body dysmorphia, orthorexia, and compulsive exercising in an ayahuasca ceremony, where I was able to see the part of me that was hurting and still hungry for love and to draw her close in my arms. In that moment, it hit me: "This body is the *only* one I get this life. I'd better treat it well. I'd better cherish it." I forgave myself for all the self-harm, criticism, and negative habits. I saw how I was *running from my power* at times by trying to keep my body small. How at times I was running from my *fire*, my mission in the world. And how I also simply wanted love. Something clicked when I saw my power was about to be unleashed as I no longer looked to the external world to provide me with validation and approval. I found a self-love that I had never known. After that I was able to do what I want without feeling shame or guilt, and I have never counted a calorie again or used harmful language when talking about my body or physical appearance. I redirected my energy into other places, and it felt amazing to graduate from this curriculum.

Ayahuasca is not the only way to conquer disordered eating or body dysmorphia and reclaim that energy and power for the good of yourself and this planet. You can use the processes in this book, too—the rituals, the gathering and sharing, the awareness, the inquiry. In this part of the book we're going to focus on ways to move back into our bodies, find love there, and reclaim our innate power by committing to a daily practice and stripping away the conditioning we have received in whatever ways we can. In the process, we will be reclaiming our bodies as spaces for joy, for happiness, for self-love, for brilliant ideas, and for allowing divine energy to shine through.

How to Begin to Heal and Transform Body Image Shame

Whether it's getting annoyed with your body sometimes, being slightly critical as you pass a mirror, making casual comments in passing about your weight, replaying past deeds in your mind, or even harboring a deep well of hidden self-hatred toward your body, the bottom line is, all of these small and not-so-small daily energy leaks around body image are siphoning away your power and your love.

These may even be ways you are subconsciously *resisting* your power and sabotaging yourself from being seen or living your purpose. This negative self-talk may prevent you from taking a stand in your life, a relationship, or your community. It could be an *epic* distraction you are unconsciously allowing that keeps you playing small, sabotages your joy, and prevents self-love from emerging.

Take a moment here. Has this internal struggle impacted your life in any way? Was there a time when you loved your body fully? Maybe you do now. Was there a time when you didn't? Did someone tell you it wasn't beautiful? That it was too big, too little, too flat, too curvy?

Do not skim over this. You may think, "I'm good. I love my body." Which is *wonderful*. But I ask you to dig a layer deeper. Our aim is to reclaim *all* the energy being leaked in this area, and some of it may be stored down in the deep subconscious, like a habit that has formed over *thousands* of years. Potentially passed down from generation to generation.

As with all our work together thus far, the first step in reprogramming your relationship to your body is to *get real about where you are at.* To become aware and to be 100 percent honest with yourself. This means noticing the micromoments when you criticize your body *and* the bodies of others, even if it's just in your mind. To notice the moments you compare bodies. Instead of getting mad at yourself for judging and criticizing, just *notice*.

This may be very difficult at first. You may get frustrated, thinking, "Damn. When I actually pay attention, I see that I spend a major amount of time worrying about my body or my appearance and judging myself." But instead of creating more suffering for yourself, consider this your first step in walking through the gates of change.

You may want to note in your journal or in your phone how many times a day you have thoughts about not liking your body, your appearance, or the appearance or bodies of others. This could include patterned thoughts of your body not being enough, or being too much, or being too big, or not being voluptuous enough. Continue keeping track this way as part of your noticing routine.

Also take note of how often you talk about your weight, food, and body—and in what context. Notice how socially acceptable it is in the West for women to discuss their body size and what they eat and ask yourself when it's necessary to engage in these conversations and why.

I got majorly chastised by one of my best friends many years ago for saying, "You look great! Did you lose weight?" She looked at me like I was a serial killer before schooling me thus: "Me looking or feeling great is not directly connected to my weight. My weight is actually pretty irrelevant when it comes to how I am doing. I am an activist. An educator for refugees. I love making mosaics and having potlucks. I am passionate about social justice. And my weight has zero impact on any of the above."

I immediately felt my eyes well with tears. I could see I was projecting my own values around weight onto her, and I realized in that moment that I had grown up in a home where food and weight were completely interwoven with my self-worth, my happiness, and my perceived value as a woman and that I still had work to do to decondition myself from these collective inherited patterns that caused me years of suffering.

So notice—without judgment—any time you mention food, not eating something, the fact you stopped with this food or that one, or the obsession with how many steps you took today. In the noticing, you may begin to ask whether spending this much time thinking and talking about your weight, body, or food intake feels like a valuable use of your time and energy. This is 100 percent up to you—it's your decision to make as to how you spend your time. You might find empowerment in sharing your food and exercise choices with your friends and family, and someone else may find they are harboring pain under their food choices. Each one of us is different, and you must honor your own healing path.

Another common thought pattern is avoiding deeper issues and wounds by obsessing about body image and food. If you feel you may fall into this pattern, you can begin to ask yourself: "Am I really worried about the fact that I ate bread last night? Or am I worried about something more profound?" If you can pull out your journal, please do. If you can sit in meditation, wonderful. Breathe into whatever is coming up. Perhaps your sudden obsession with your carb intake or the fact you skipped Pilates class is about something else. Allow this moment to be a portal for looking into something deeper that's stirring inside of you.

Perhaps, when you travel all the way down there, you will hear something buried under the food or body anxieties such as: "I'll never get married. Especially if I eat pasta." Then you can see it is not really about the pasta, but about the desire for love. About the desire to feel valued as a woman in a society that tells us marriage is a marker of value.

If and when you can find clear insights hiding under thoughts about food or body image, try to feel the part of you beneath the surface thoughts, the one that wants love. Be compassionate with her. Love her and accept her. Tell her it's okay to want love and sit with whatever comes up. There may be tears. Anger may surface. Let everything out and begin to allow your true heart to show up, the you that is infinite, magnetic, and hidden under all the bullshit.

This is how transformation happens. When we don't shove our feelings and small hurts under the rug but instead allow them to point to a place inside that is asking for our help, then we can sit with those parts of ourselves. We look at them. We open to them and allow the poison and the pain to turn into a deep compassion for ourselves and for all the experiences that have made us who we are.

This all happens within. No pill can do this whole process for you. No crystal wand or magic spell will rid you of your feelings and issues. It is within your human experience to contemplate, to uncover, to purge, to unravel, and to be reborn through your own work. Yes, I can teach you practices—as can many others. But only you have the power to make the internal shifts.

Another reason some of the aforementioned symptoms associated with food and the body arise is because we are attempting to find control. For kids who had chaotic childhoods, food intake is a simple way to bring about a sense of control and comfort or to create a space that distracts from feelings of pain and shame and guilt. Recently I was sitting with a client who told me, "I keep going to do the practices you sent me. And then I end up watching TV and snacking the minute I sit down to begin." She walked me through the moment when, instead of letting herself feel her heart's true longing, she walked to the kitchen and grabbed some nuts. Then she went back for peanut butter. Then chocolate. Then more peanut butter.

I replied, "This is great! You are aware of what you're doing. And we are staring at the symptom of a deeper wound. This is an opportunity, if we take it." She agreed to dive into it further. As we worked together, she eventually acknowledged what it was she was truly hungry for and what she was avoiding. Turns out that still, at age twenty-seven, she was hungry for the love of her father, whom she'd lost to a divorce at fourteen. Turns out she was also running from her desire to start a climate-change aid organization. I led her back into her heart, where the feelings were waiting for her to feel them, to contemplate them, to examine them, and to express them. Then she committed to get back into her body with breath work and contemplation and dance practices, so her mind would stop constantly calling her to snacking and other distractions. This way she could begin to take action in the world from that authentic place.

I have had other clients who don't want to get out of their heads and into their bodies because their bodies feel unsafe, like crime scenes left gathering dust, ghosts lingering in the shadows. There are too many wild feelings and memories running around in there. For them, it feels so much easier to stay immersed in the to-do lists, the planning, the future tripping—*thinking, not feeling*. Meaning a life in the head and not in the current moment, in the body, where there may be pain, anxiety, sadness, and even excitement to be present with.

Training yourself to deeply feel again and to trust your body means you regain access to the *present*. Where you're able to *feel* music deeply in your soul or the sun shining on your face. Where a compliment can hit your heart like gold.

When we live in the past and future—in the head—then we miss *all* those presents. Love does not live in the head; it lives in the heart. So when we're not home in our body, we are missing out on love.

I know that it's 100 percent possible to live without that voice inside, constantly criticizing and bringing you down in moments where you could be enjoying *life*. To not be sitting at parties, dinners, and birthdays looking happy on the outside but hating yourself on the inside. To do this, again, we must get real and journey into the depths without judgment. This is how we transform our body-image shame into a celebration of how amazing we truly are.

Rewrite Your Body Programming

When it comes to our bodies, most of us inherited a default way of seeing that is antiquated and negatively biased toward this sacred vessel.

For example, if you grew up in the US, it could be that you rarely saw anyone with your skin color and body type reflected on TV shows, movies, and in magazines. Your tiny child brain was being programmed from a young age with subtle and not-so-subtle messaging saying: "You will be loved and valued only if you look like [*insert fave model or movie star here*]."

Chances are, this programming impacts your relationship to your self-image, influencing how you wear your hair, how you dress, and how you view yourself to this day. But what if having your barometer for sexiness set by the media just doesn't feel like *you*? I want to help you get to a place where what is sexy and beautiful when it comes to your body is something that *you* get to curate and let morph from day to day.

This is completely possible. All it takes is cultivating the kind of awareness we have been practicing and doing the work of moving past your blocks.

What I mean is, if you wake up every morning and do not *consciously* put the channel of your inner radio onto the station of your choosing, you will just stay on the free government channel with all its controlling, capitalist advertising messages. The good news is, once you begin this internal work, it's never too late to reprogram yourself from the oppressive old narratives to ones that feel nourishing and supportive and juicy as fuck.

Remember, you are doing this work for all the women who couldn't and who still can't. As you do your work, you are paving the way for future generations of women to *not* have this body programming in their minds. This work you do for you is truly an act of service to the world.

What if instead of letting your parents or society program your mind, you found a way back to your soul's deep inner knowing? The knowledge and wisdom that is inside you. An inner knowing that is so profound it has the power to evaporate the societal programming like a laser beam. What if you could access that inner knowing?

You might free up enough head and heart space to create a solution to a huge world problem. You might find yourself laughing more. You might feel more peace in your body and less worry. You might write an amazing screenplay. You might walk through the world as an example of someone embodied and in their power, who doesn't look like the cookie-cutter version of perfection we have been fed. And who knows whom you may inspire from that place?

Anything is possible when you reclaim your internal state, your well-being, and, most of all, your *body*.

Reclaim the Body, Reclaim the Pussy

When we begin to think about the internalized shame and pain associated with the female body, we cannot skip over the place that perhaps holds the most guilt and fear of all . . . the part that has been named "private" and covered and hidden away under nylon panties and tight thongs, stripped with hot wax and plastic razors. Call it your pussy. Your yoni. Your cunt. Your vulva. Call it what you will. But just call it! We can't fully reclaim our trust and dialogue with our body if we don't acknowledge the pussy. And even if you don't have one, this does not mean you can't be on the team to honor and support the healing of this physical and energetic space that has been greatly hidden and abused and to call on its power for yourself.

In certain tantric traditions they say the goddesses live in there and are waiting to be awakened! We can interpret this as meaning we have a magical tool hidden inside, a compass or secret oracle, that we can touch base with anytime if we so choose. Ever since I learned this, whenever I need to make a big decision or when I am confused about something, I feel into my cervix. *Not my head.* Remember, the mind is conditioned by past traumas, family patterns, society's ideas—it's been programmed by the outside. Dropping deeper in, down to the cervix, as abstract as that may sound, is a way to connect to a very ancient part of yourself, a profound inner wisdom.

Literally speaking, the cervix is the lower portion of the uterus. It is approximately two inches long, and it's tubular in shape. But it also represents an energetic point inside of you, whether you have a physical cervix or not. In Chinese medicine this point is connected to the heart. Which is why when you have sex and someone touches your cervix, you may feel a heart opening. You may even start to cry—which totally makes sense, when you consider that most of us have a lot of stored tension and pain and shame there. We will get into how to move that in a moment. If you don't have a physical cervix, you can connect to this energy point in your subtle body system, breathing it open, visualizing it, and connecting with its power.

A new life has the ability to enter the body there. A very magical thing, *the creation of another human*, happens in this place. There is much power in that. And the cervix as a direct portal to the divine has been written about in spiritual texts for thousands of years. It is no wonder the modern church has tried to control women's bodies for so long—we have a *divine portal* to the mystery of infinity between our legs. For the church to be unable to control something so uncertain, so wild, is a threat. The male leaders of organized religion throughout time have spread the message that in order to know the divine you have to go through them, so of course they have vilified this direct dial-up.

In Sanskrit, the word *yoni*, relating to the vulva in general, means "sacred temple." In many tantric traditions this part of the woman is *revered*. The juices secreted there are considered to be the *amrita*, or nectar of the gods, in Sanskrit.

Imagine walking through life knowing you had an ancient device inside of you that's way more intelligent than your iPhone. But you get access to it only with deep practice and by wooing that wise energy out of hiding, facing any shame or guilt blocking the dialogue from occurring.

If you make love without this deeper part of yourself *open* and in tune, you'll be making love or fucking on the surface, superficially. From the mind and from the physical body, but *not* from the soul or spirit or ground of your being. We'll discuss this in more depth in the next chapter, but this type of sex may leave you feeling empty, bored, sad, and disillusioned. When you start a dialogue with your cervix is when you get to have sex that connects to deep truth, wisdom, and the infinity of creation. And *that* is how you fuck like a goddess.

The reawakening of this sacred portal happens over time. You can't just plug it in, turn it on, or flip a switch. If you've heard it called evil, "too much," or dirty, it will take practice and *patience* and healing to bring it back online and undo the conditioning and wounding lying dormant there. But reclaiming this part of yourself is an important piece of coming home to your body, and it requires its own deep act.

Here is how to begin:

- **Daily listening.** Take five minutes a day to breathe into your cervix and start to attempt to feel it. Imagine a red light in there, like a pilot light or a little flame. With each breath you take, imagine the light becoming bigger. And then stop to sense what that feels like. In the same way you can often feel your heart in a meditation, not with your hand, but with energy, feel into the cervix. What does it feel like in there? Is there a warmth? A tingle?

- **Attention.** Notice how your heart and your cervix feel when you meet someone you may be interested in romantically or someone you are partnered with, and then notice the connection between those two parts of your body. Or notice how the heart and cervix feel when your partner says something yummy to you or when they say something annoying. Begin to learn this language by simply noticing. It's subtle at times and more powerful at others.

- **Sex.** Begin listening here. For example, if it is dry down there, it may mean that the heart and the cervix are not connected. Unless you have a medical issue or even dehydration, dryness may be a signal that the mind is too busy and more presence, breath, and connection are required. It could also be a signal that this person or moment is not a match. Or that more foreplay is needed to open you more deeply to the moment and trust and surrender. This inner inquiry while in the sexual moment can be very helpful as you begin to understand the subtle language within.

Once I was dating an Adonis-looking neoshaman with a beautiful chiseled body and a lot of spiritual quotes up his sleeve. And while I knew we weren't exactly soul mates, it had been a *while* since I'd had any love, and I went for it. When he offered to pick me up for dinner, then pretended he forgot something at his place and casually asked if we could stop in, I could totally see through his ploy...but I said yes.

Within minutes he had us sitting together on the floor in a meditation position. Inside, I was laughing the whole time, because, well, he was being so obvious! He proceeded to offer me rapé (a South American tobacco snuff used traditionally in ceremony, not on dates) and then asked me to do energy work on him so he could feel my powers. I was witnessing this whole scene with an inner chuckle; it seemed harmless, like a story I would tell my friends with laughter.

Soon after our meditation, my powers must have gotten to him, because he was all over me, kissing me, telling me he felt my inner goddess, and pulling my clothes off. I couldn't take him seriously, but at the time I thought it would be a harmless hookup.

But guess what? My yoni had other ideas! After we hooked up, I came down with bacterial vaginosis for the first time ever. It was extremely painful. It was as if my yoni was saying, "Honey, you cannot put an unconscious man, one who just wants to use your body, in your sacred temple anymore." I listened to her, and I told him I didn't want to see him again. Then I took care of myself and promised my body I would not repeat that lesson.

Several years later I found out he was stalking several women in the area and had been accused of sexual assault. I was floored. Perhaps my body had protected me from going any further with this man.

Our body does indeed contain its own oracle, which will bring you home to your innate power and wisdom again and again.

THE TRANSFORMATIONAL WORK: THE BODY

You can keep doing the embodied healing and transformational work I've outlined for anything that came up in this chapter around your body. Remember, you may feel resistance—and if you find yourself shying away from an exercise, then perhaps it's time to do it. But even just reading the words in this chapter has created a shift in your awareness that will be mirrored around you.

Body Image Check-In

First, let's take inventory to see where you currently are in your relationship to your body. Create a sacred space for yourself. Then jot down responses to the prompts below in your journal. You can be as brief or write for as long as you like. This list is simply to help you get clear.

- When am I triggered when it comes to my body?
- What are the stories I tell myself about my body?
- When do I have moments of comparison with other women and their bodies?
- When do I restrict food or change my eating habits?
- When do I overeat or binge?
- What did my parents teach me about food?
- What did my parents teach me about my body?

- What part(s) of my body do I feel shame about?

- When I feel too big or fat, what do I usually do?

These answers will point you in the direction of any blocks you are holding—where there is a pocket of still-stuck pain, where shame or fear still burns through your battery power. Then you can use the embodiment practices I outlined to go into these areas more deeply. Now you can begin to *face* the things that are holding the most *charge* or *zing*, so you can work on releasing and integrating them.

Storytelling Ritual

Storytelling with intention is a ritualistic way to process, move through, contemplate, and learn from our life lessons. It's ancient and marks a way as humans we have always healed and connected. Reclaiming the storytelling space from passive consumption of TV and film into a space of active participation can be very healing.

Make a time to gather with one or two trusted and close friends whom you feel safe with, with the collective intention to share your stories about your body, your journey with your body, and the comedy and/or tragedy you have perhaps experienced in this life. (Possible topics: first sex, menstrual cycle, a triumph of self-hate, et cetera.) You can use the questions from the Body Image Check-In to spark inspiration. And please don't run from this one. It will be healing, I promise. Prepare some tea, light a candle, and get cozy.

First, set a timer for each share. It could be fifteen minutes, twenty, or even thirty. And remind one another to simply *listen* when someone is speaking—no cross talk. You might feel the impulse to say, "OMG, that happened to me too!" Or you may want to comfort your friend and rub her back if she cries. But the purpose of this ritual is to simply allow one another to be seen and to shed any emotions that come up without interruption. The listeners need to actively hold space for this. To be present. To breathe with the speaker's pain as it bubbles up and not attempt to fix and console. It is the job of each of you to give your full attention to whomever is sharing at that moment.

Before you begin, have everybody state that nothing shared will be discussed outside this space. Once everyone has shared, you can close the ritual by blowing out your candle. Put on some music to move the energy in the room. You can light some incense. Open a window. Dance it out. And just let it all go.

By digging deep into all areas of our life, we will indeed see where there are lessons to still benefit from, fears to face, moments to mourn, and space to be made. When we dig deep, we see it's not our fault at all—we are not victims of circumstance but of a set of beliefs and patterns dictated by the world we live in. And it's up to us to change those patterns, for ourselves and the generations to come. We have that power. In our own bodies. With our choices. We have the ability to make change. To pull down the masks. To breathe a sigh of relief and say, "You too?" And to begin to transform the pain into love.

HOW TO LOVE
LIKE A GODDESS

I let myself love. And be loved.

In ways I have never seen before on TV, in movies.

I let myself be loved as I am. Now. Here.

With all my wounds open,

All my fucked-up bits showing.

I let this be more healing than any ceremony I have done.

Any retreat. Any meditation. Any therapy session!

I allow it to create wholeness.

To tell my soul that there is no need to hide or contract or retract
or put a mask on.

That I am lovable *as is*!

I let myself feel relief.

Hiding all those parts is exhausting.

It takes glasses of wine. It takes sentences like "I am fine."

It takes big gulps and tightness in the jaw, holding it all together.

When I find myself being loved, even in the moments
I am fighting demons,

Dancing with shadows, I will stop!

I will say "Thank you" to the heavens! Praise the miracle that it is.

Teach my nervous system in that moment:

This is what love feels like.

Love that is unconditional.

Love that doesn't judge how fucked up I may be.

This is real love.

HEALING AND TRANSFORMATION take *time*. Time to meditate. To tune in. To listen and observe. However, advances in technology often mean that in our modern world, everything is speeding up, while internally some of us are attempting to slow down. And one place this modern speed change is apparent is in the realm of dating, intimacy, and sex.

Dating apps may give dating, sex, and connection a disposable quality. A direct message or a "like" can be all it takes to hook up. And if it doesn't work out? There is a pervading spirit infiltrating the collective: "Ghost 'em, block 'em, and move on." In today's world, the onslaught of smartphones, apps, social media, and fast living can deter the process of deep connection. It can be fun to live in this speedy world, but does it feel nourishing to the spirit? Does it create a sense of emotional safety or intimate connection? Does it equal depth? Not always. Our collective hunger causes us to unconsciously chase naturally occurring chemicals released in the brain during pleasurable situations, motivating us to repeat that behavior with the promise of another reward. The people who made the apps know we get a hit every time we get a "like." Our seemingly innocent nervous systems, which just want us to love and be loved, have been hacked by apps, websites, TV, ads, et cetera. Not to imply that we are *victims* of technology, but our systems are experiencing a big transition without a clear map as to how to consciously navigate these changing waters.

The technological advances in the last few decades have changed the entire landscape of modern relationships. On the dating scene, yes, but even within committed marriages people now have the constant temptation of getting a quick dopamine hit via Facebook "likes" or messages, instead of doing the work of maintaining deep intimacy with a spouse, which may not provide a quick hit of pleasure. If the friend or lover you're hanging out with isn't sparking enough feel-good hormones, you may unconsciously pick up your phone and look for those hits on social media, in texts, or in your emails instead, just to get a dose of that chemical the divine designed to create connection between two humans. These moments of unconscious behaviors draw us further away from the type of love that soothes the spirit, that provides a sense of deep belonging and connection to source. And yet this form of avoidance of love and depth has become completely socially acceptable, as phones grace dinner tables and bedsides and seem to be glued to our palms.

So how do we create a five-course feast of deep connection in a fast-food, quickie world? And as technology advances, how do we begin to allow for the advancement of the way we experience love and connection—instead of staying stuck in what the media has fed us our whole lives about what relationships are "supposed" to look like and be like? How do we trust that it's okay to become increasingly more vulnerable, less masked, less full of societal conditioning, less tied to outdated modes of being? How do we progress into more evolved ways of loving when social media and fast-paced materialist living have made connection available as a superficial and throwaway commodity?

To allow our collective healing to occur, we must investigate the moments we avoid it. We must be honest about what we are truly craving underneath the surface cravings of phone, snacks, alcohol, sugar, and TV. You know a deeper hunger is there. As we find the courage to ask these questions, we reclaim our power—our sexual energy, our creativity—and know it at its source. To do this we must take a dive into our internal muck, perhaps get a bit dirty as we swim through it, and come out the other side victorious.

The system that conditioned how we relate to each other as humans is evolving past outdated and oppressive unconsciousness. We are at a crucial time in our evolution; our future is uncertain. Our shared history is full of suffering, pain, competition, and exploitation, yet also there is beauty, innovation, and boundless creativity throughout time. Perhaps a *good* thing about our sped-up twenty-first-century world is that information is traveling much faster than ever—meaning that evolution has the ability to happen much faster, too, if we choose to engage with it in such a way. When it comes to romantic relationships, sex, and commitment, we can look through a new lens and ask ourselves:

If I hadn't grown up watching my parents as a model for relationship...

If the way my parents loved me wasn't how I learned love...

If religion and movies and TV shows didn't shape what I think love is...

How would I love then?

How would I make love then?

In this chapter you may redefine, or expand upon, the way you date, the way you have sex, and the way you love. This is for everyone, whether you are single, married, or otherwise partnered. There is always more depth to be found.

My Journey of Learning to Love and Be Loved

I've always marched to the beat of my own drum when it comes to relationships—or so I thought. In the past few years I have seen how my parents' patterns around love played out unconsciously in many of my adult relationships. And also how the media, the stories I had been fed since I was a kid, and the religious and cultural ideas surrounding me created rigid and stale models and conditioning around two of the most glorious elements human life has to offer: sex and love.

From my vantage point, I deduced that both of my parents love *love* more than anything. Throughout my life, I have watched them each love deeply and also have their hearts broken many times. Every time I experienced one of their heart-cracking-open moments, it tore my own heart open, too. I witnessed them fight with their lovers and battle tragic fallout from their divorces. They have *six* divorces between them. I also saw their worlds blossom open when they fell in love. When my mom met my stepdad, she sat me down and said, "I've met my soul mate." I was shocked, at fifteen, not having met the man whom she was alerting me would be an addition to our world. But I saw her soul had come alive. My mom took me through Love School, through the lens of her own experience.

I heard my father, meanwhile, use the words "She's the love of my life!" more times than I can remember. I feel he has meant it each time; I sense in him, as well, the deep desire to love and be loved. Whenever this desire was followed by yet another breakup or divorce, my heart broke at seeing him sad. Through my parents, I came to begin to understand loving. I began to relate to that moment when everything feels possible and we dive into our deepest human desire to love and be loved. When we feel the inherent divinity that we are, which seems to surface when we are "in love."

I had my first boyfriend in kindergarten, chasing connection while almost still in diapers, it seemed. Followed by my first sexual experience in seventh grade, while still wearing braces on my teeth, under fairy lights and a mosquito-net-covered bed with two other cheerleaders. I accepted at this point that I was bisexual, or pansexual (though I didn't yet know that term), or that I simply loved to love. Gender felt arbitrary when applied to my sexuality. And though I was shamed and ostracized for this view, even in middle school in 1996 in Marietta, Georgia, it still felt most natural to me to kiss boys and girls, of any color or age. I just wanted to express love. I was curious. I knew somewhere in my soul that there was more to loving than what the Disney movies and TV shows had shown me.

Besides the cultural programming, the drama and passion around love I inherited from the Brazilian side of my family via my father brought intensity after each breakup, as well as a mimicking of my father's behavior of having multiple lovers and being driven by love. (Something that throughout history was deemed a bit more ordinary and acceptable for men, especially in Latin cultures, where the Casanova archetype emerges from. Giacomo Casanova was an Italian man known for his complex and elaborate love life and many lovers.) In seventh grade, three different boys brought me Valentine's Day gifts: a dozen roses, a box of chocolates, poetry—and I had to choose which one I wanted. This pattern replayed throughout the years, until I healed and integrated the promiscuous spirit of my teens and twenties into something more evolved and empowered.

In order to launch this piece of my healing, the first thing I decided to do was to take some time away from dating. I wanted to make space to pave a new way for myself that was drama free and linked to a new phase of evolution of love for my own family and self.

During this time of self-healing with love, I apologized to the people I had hurt, either in person or in meditation. I cried many tears—for the times I had gotten myself into situations that led to abuse because of my craving for love and my wild curiosity about love and sex; for the times I had hurt others; for my own unconscious behavior. I cried for the part of me that was scared of deep and vulnerable love. I also knew that to graduate from these deeply ingrained familial and societal patterns, I had to face all my own shadows.

In the middle of this healing process, I sat in a series of workshops about love and intimacy, and I began to physically experience the walls I had constructed around my heart, like painful, hard, calcified blocks preventing me from experiencing deep and present love. I also faced any lingering resentment I had toward cis men, all my feminist postpatriarchal anger, anger toward my father, and any other hurts I had stored away. In this realization, I saw that one of my biggest lessons in this lifetime is to stand *with* men and help heal our collective wounds together instead of seeing them as the enemy.

When this journey began, I was still harboring a lot of anger that I didn't even know was in me. In these workshops, I would scream and yell at the man standing in front of me, unleashing all my past hurts onto him. He was instructed to hold my emotions and stay strong. One time I screamed so fiercely, like a wild beast, that the man in front of me jumped back as if he was running from a fire. I saw his eyes well with tears—and *my* eyes are full of tears as I write this. Why? First, because it wasn't his responsibility to hold my pain. And second, because the unexpressed and displaced rage and pain from wounding that so many of us carry in our bodies run deep. All the times we didn't speak up, didn't honor our bodies, or were abused or mistreated. Often it feels terrifying to face these wounds, and often we lack the tools. But if we don't process the wounds, each time we go on a date or make love to our spouse, this unspoken pain is like a dark cloud hanging over the scene. And in those moments there is an opportunity to heal, through intimacy.

In order to welcome healthy love into my life, I had to face it *all*. Otherwise I would bring it to each and every new relationship, like a bag of rotten corpses. The following stretch of months of not dating and no sex were a healing experience in my heart like nothing I have ever been through. With no booze to numb my sadness. No cheating. No passionate yelling. I was doing my work. Looking at my shadows, and healing myself. All in the name of clearing the blocks that were preventing me from receiving real, deep, and nourishing love.

One of my favorite Rumi quotes is: "Your task is not to seek for love, but merely to seek and find all the barriers within yourself that you have built against it." And that is what was happening to me. The walls around my heart built by patterns, fear, and past experiences were crumbling down. This time I did not escape into drama. I did not escape into work or exercise, alcohol or sugar. Though the pain, anxiety, and sadness felt almost unbearable at times, I stuck with it anyway. I expressed it and moved through it. I meditated, breathed, took baths, cried, wrote, shared with loved ones, practiced rituals, sat in silence, went on retreat, sat in ceremonies, and eventually, through time and practice, a heaviness I had felt in my heart my whole life lifted.

Shifting old patterns that we've inherited through our families or the collective consciousness can feel like stopping a freight train at times: it may take a while to come to a complete stop, but inch by inch, the wheels gradually stop turning. And from here, this calm place of stillness, you get to *choose* what kind of love you want—

instead of repeating programmed patterns and ways of being that you inherited or were conditioned into. This is where love finds freedom.

What's Your Love Story?

When we start questioning the status quo and noticing that we have outgrown the old ways, we are paving the new road for new ways of being and loving. We can't look to old models as examples. We must create fresh ones. In investigating your unique relationship patterns, you can embark on this journey of creating and making space for the love you crave.

The first step is always awareness. It's the getting-real part. Feeling what is present. Identifying the patterns in real time. This is the part that means taking off the blinders and being willing to see your own blind spots. Whether that means eliminating any ways you numb or check out of the present moment and seeing what emerges on your own or spending more time being present or sitting with a coach or a therapist, there is a moment when we are called to say: "I am ready to remove all barriers to love, even though it will mean I have to do the hard work of noticing the barriers first, tending the wounds, and beginning the demolition process."

The problem with looking simply to external examples for the kind of relationships we want is that they often fail us. We may look to two celebrities who seem super happy and successful, only to find them getting a divorce down the line. We may construct our idea of love on the basis of a hodgepodge of romantic films, only to realize that the carefully written plots and twists and turns and musical touches are designed to evoke the feelings we are seeking. At this time on the planet we need to create new examples of what relationships can look like, relationships that are as bold and courageous and messy as they are beautiful. Ones that don't fit the old paradigm, because we no longer fit it either.

If you look back to the 1950s, perhaps to your grandparents, you may see very traditional and old-fashioned gender roles. And perhaps a lot of alcohol, unconsciously used to keep feelings at bay, stress levels down, and households calm. One of my grandfathers was in the navy, loved a good martini, and probably never spoke about his feelings to anyone. My grandma was beautiful and well groomed, and she died early of lung cancer. In traditional Chinese medicine, the lungs are where we store grief, and I can only wonder what sadness my grandma had been holding her whole life. She was a housewife who perhaps didn't have space to feel her feelings in communion with other women, to practice rituals, and to let go into her body and spirit, and she was married to a man who likely wasn't very present or available emotionally for her.

Thank goddess for the 1960s and the '70s and the seismic shifts and vast cultural rebellion of the free love movement, the cultural emergence of psychedelics, and the antiwar, anti-establishment sentiments that ensued. We owe much of our progress to the rebellion of this generation, which was brought up by parents stuck in cultural, social, political, and spiritual patterns that were rapidly becoming outdated. And things kept changing. By the time the '80s came around, many women were working full time while also raising children and hitting up *Jane Fonda's Workout* like nobody's business. In many places, the notion that a woman needed a man as a provider began to be turned on its head.

It may have been subconscious, but the modern woman's need for a man changed. (There are many extensive books on this subject, a few of which I recommend on my site.) The fact that women were

finally beginning to be seen as equals in many parts of the world—
of course, not all of them—was ultimately positive, though as with
any change, there are growing pains, confusion, and a time of transition that can be awkward and clumsy.

As a result of this great reshuffling of gender roles, you could say
that in some ways we've arrived in 2020 with a lot of possibility in
terms of the structures of family and relationships and gender. Not
that there isn't a *long* way to go in terms of gender equality, LGBTQ
rights, and women's rights in many parts of the world, including
in the West. But for many of us, we can choose how we relate to
one another and what roles we take in relationships and marriages.
Though gender nonconformity, fluidity, and nonbinary expression
have existed throughout time, in some places in the world perhaps
it's the first time in history that education, openness, and acceptance are beginning to emerge about these aspects of being. Seeds
are being planted, old views are being overturned, and a new time
is dawning for the future of sex and relationships.

The possibilities from this point for the collective and the individual are endless. The tricky part now may be looking inside yourself
and finding what feels right for *you*. How do you dig underneath
the history, the past hurts, the patterning, and the conditioning and
find the part of you that even knows how to give and receive love
and then decide how that looks? This is a beautiful aspect of each
of our journeys of self-discovery—the creation of our own personal
art through how we love, and make love, and relate to one another.

Perhaps as we are evolving we can make space for relationship—
not simply for convenience, comfort, or the seeking of nuclear
family, but as a sacred vehicle for transformation, a space to transform in, to face our fears in, to see our truth mirrored in. If as a
collective we are examining why we do what we do, then let us

examine this area, too. Why we couple, why we love, why many of us still convene together in pairs in homes set apart from others. If we can allow for the next phase of our collective growth and see the partner as our sacred mirror, the crucible for our awakening, then imagine the possibilities.

Receiving Love

The way you receive love is equally important as the way you give love. Receiving love means how deeply you can feel love dancing throughout your body, how deeply you can feel your partner's presence within you. Your ability to receive it fully determines how much joy and nourishment you can take in from love. This ability to feel love transcends romance. It is a deep love that exists within each of us, if we choose to access it and transform that which prohibits it.

Think back to a time in your life where you didn't know you had it so good. Maybe there was a really wonderful human who loved and cherished you, but you didn't see it. Or maybe people were telling you how incredibly beautiful and smart you are, but you couldn't feel it. Pinpoint one moment like this, and let's sit with it.

Why was it that you couldn't feel into the depth of the love available to you? Or appreciate the depth of your own radiance? Could it be that a part of you was still closed off as a result of the hurts of the past and was creating a barrier between you and love? Could it be that you subconsciously felt undeserving?

When we are closed to receiving, it doesn't matter how wonderful the love is or how beautiful we are—we just can't feel it. Love *wants* to move through us. But so often we are stuck in our heads, tripping out on stories about our future or lost deep in the shadows of our past hurts, and we simply do not have the capacity to receive.

Because the only place we can receive love is in the present moment.

So whether you're sitting opposite your long-term partner or you're on a first date, actually being *with* the person in front of you is *essential* to you opening to their love. This means feeling the present, opening to it, and allowing it to move through you, even when you can't control it. Learning to receive the love in front of you is an art, a process, and a practice.

First, it means making space. We do this by once again getting real about what hurts and what has happened in the past. We do this by expressing old feelings and hurts, moving them *through* our bodies. By acknowledging our deepest yearnings for love and being unashamed to voice them. By letting go of control and being willing to free-fall into the vast unknown of potential love.

Ultimately, learning how to deeply *feel* is how we begin to deeply receive. This is a key part of what I teach with embodiment practices using breath and sound and movement, like the ones you can listen to guided by me on the website. I also encourage radical self-expression. Dancing. Raging. Screaming. Lying down in a star shape on the ground and crying. Often the more we can express, the more we loosen and open, and the more space we create for love. It can feel scary and vulnerable, but when the dust of past hurts is cleared and when the heart is open again, it can also feel amazing. Like a return to love. A deep sigh. Like coming home.

One way I know that I am not in receiving mode, and perhaps my heart is closed, is when I haven't cried tears of gratitude in a while. In these moments, I sense I have lost touch with my heart and probably am in survival mode or in go-go-go mode, places from which it's so much harder to receive.

To address this, I created what I call my Surrender Saturday practice. On such days, I do all the things I know connect me to my heart. I abandon my to-do list. I listen to evocative music that will help tears to drip from my eyes. I take inventory of all that I have and become appreciative. I feel the feelings that I haven't had the space to feel all week. I just *melt*. And in this practice, I create a new opening for love.

Crafting this space for yourself will be part of your transformation in chapter 8. But for now, let's talk some more about giving and receiving in the realm of sex.

How to Fuck: With Your Mind, Body, and Soul

There is a clear difference between casual sex, where it's all about the physical act, and an experience where hearts and souls and energy bodies are fully awake and aligned and alive.

I have experienced both, plus many shades in between, and chances are you have, too.

The second kind of sexual experience leaves you feeling refreshed, open, connected to source, and perhaps even high on life. Also deeply connected to yourself and to your partner. Your old patterns and stories that are usually running through your mind may have gone quiet for a while. Perhaps you can get up and walk to the bathroom without putting on a robe. Let your hair be wild. Not care if you have BO. Perhaps you have deeply relaxed.

You are a radiant *being* after this deeper kind of sex. The divine source energy of creation is flowing through you to the point that you have *become* one with it.

On the flip side, if you are having unconscious sex, maybe while you are tipsy or a little drunk, perhaps in a one-night stand that you aren't super excited about, you may first get a dose of adrenaline. "Oooh, I am doing something wild! This is fun!" This adrenaline will carry you through the initial part of the experience and may be additionally fueled by any alcohol in your system. A cocktail of chemicals is flowing freely through your body, bringing you to the moment of lovemaking perhaps without your thinking twice. This kind of sexual experience may be wild, rough, messy, intense, and passionate, but it does not often involve your heart and soul. Maybe there's a little eye contact, or maybe that's too intimate. Afterward, the mood may shift. Maybe there's some cuddling, maybe not. Maybe it's awkward.

Does your heart feel full? Do you feel like a radiant piece of divinity? Are you left feeling empowered? Or drained? Has the adrenaline worn off? And how does it feel a few days later? Still exciting, or kind of "meh"?

I'm not saying either kind of sex is "better." I have leaned on unconscious sex during phases of my life when I was bored, lonely, curious, exploring new things, or simply craving connection. This kind of sex at times was also me experimenting with operating outside of society's rules of what was okay for women. I was rebelling against a system that felt old and crunchy. I imagined there was an inner pagan wild woman in me who just wanted to be free! To make love in fields with strangers, as in some ancient rituals, and to bless the earth with my body.

And it was liberating. To have totally sober sex with someone I barely knew was exhilarating. I would challenge myself to see if and when I checked out or disassociated during the sex, hyperaware because I was sober. Was it because this person was off? Was it because I didn't really want sex?

Years back, I remember being in San Francisco and chatting with a French tech guy. At the time I had been exploring conscious kink and was feeling really adventurous. I felt safe to be quite open with people about what I was looking for, and I went to meet this Frenchman for a coffee. He was gentle and sweet, and we went to his apartment and had wonderful, connected sex. No booze. Sunlight bathed the whole room. I had multiple orgasms. There were no expectations, there was no emotional hangover, and I left feeling *full*-power me, calm, peaceful, and radiant. But not all attempts at more casual sex were so expansive. Others were draining, compromising, and even a bit frightful.

Throughout my short but potent phase of exploring more casual sex, there were times I had many orgasms in experiences with new people, because I felt safe, and times I did not feel safe or have orgasms. There were times I felt held and safe because I wasn't checking out with substances. When I challenged myself to be sober and present, I learned to trust *myself* to know when it was safe to open and when it wasn't. I share this, not to encourage you or not encourage you to have casual sex, but rather to illustrate that casual sex can be conscious sex too, when you are *aware* of your baggage, your patterns, and your projections and when you are willing to show up, sober, and real, and whole, as *you*. Then, this moment of authentic connection can be deeply healing.

The more I healed myself, though, the less I found I had the time or energy for unconscious sex and the emotional, mental, and spiritual hangovers or internal self-talk that often followed. My desires turned toward more spiritual, sacred partnerships, and a transition occurred. During this change, my own solo sex practice became strong, and I didn't feel hungry for sex with people when there was not a deep container in place. For the times when I haven't wanted to have sex with another person, but because I was deep in my own healing process and very raw or tender, I learned how to have sacred sex with myself, instead of waiting for the next suitor to appear or seeking one out.

As with everything, and as I've mentioned, we've been fed an idea of what sex looks like by TV, movies, and advertising. Chances are our parents and sex ed classes at school gave us the lowdown on what sex is technically "for" (making babies, *not* just pleasure). And it's likely we have spent most of our lives emulating what we saw, without consciously exploring the kind of sex we really want. So often it's lights out, under sheets, in the dark... The truth is, there are one million ways to make love. To have sex. To fuck. There are ways that do not even involve physical touch. Most of us have not explored the range of possibilities here, simply because we weren't taught how. As we open, as we heal, as we grow, the doors to the infinite open, and we are reminded of our potential.

Sexual Alchemy

When we reveal the truth of who we are in our sexual experiences, it can help to heal and transform us in really deep ways. When we open profoundly, our pains, our fears, our projections, our hopes, and our desires all rise to the surface. And if we have courage, we can let these moments be incredibly transformative ones, ones where instead of shutting down, we experience a type of rebirth.

As mentioned, this means practicing discernment as to whom you want to have share in your soul-shaking, ancestral-pattern-healing, neurosis-baring, transformative sexual experience. Enter this type of union with caution: not only can it be extraordinarily terrifying to open yourself up and allow all of those things to surface, but you will be receiving and experiencing all of that from your partner as well. And for that you need trust, and you need to be ready to face whatever shadows and demons your partner may bring and not run for the hills when they open.

Not everyone wants or is ready for such a wide-open, exposed, raw, messy, transformative, karmic clearing sexual experience. It is one that can refresh your entire existence, purify your patterns, free you, and let you feel seen in ways that you rarely are. It is for deep divers on the journey. It is written about in many ancient texts. And it is terrifying, as you must look at all your broken bits, your fucked-up parts, and your patterns and love past them, let yourself be loved in spite of them. It is radical, and it is not for the faint of heart.

In order to even begin to embark on this phase of your own personal alchemical transformation, first it's about that *container*, that proverbial bowl, cauldron, or sacred space that holds the magic between two people. As we know, without a solid container, magic can rarely happen. It is the trust between two people that creates a solid ground for this kind of magic to be possible. So does time. So does actual space.

Safety and trust are key for this type of deep work to occur. You definitely can't rush a soul-healing orgasmic experience or even pencil it into your agenda. And you probably can't have one in your childhood bedroom while visiting your parents for Christmas. You need to set a sacred space, like you would for any ritual. Your action can be as simple as lighting one candle. Taking a bath or shower with intention beforehand. Putting on a silk kimono or whatever feels good to *you*. Putting the phones away. Not speaking about the mundane for that time. Burning a little incense. Putting on some music that feels really good.

This experience can be a part of your divine healing practice, your daily art, and the wonderful adventure of discovering *you* under the patterns, habits, fears, desires, and mind's incessant chatter. Once you claim this space with intent and power and you bring a little more sacredness to the sexual act, the container of the sexual experience will begin to respond to you. It will become *magical*, perhaps more confronting, more intense, and ultimately more transformative.

When I have cocreated deeply intentional sexual experiences, *magic* has happened. I've seen stars in the room. Orbs of energy. My body has dissolved into light. I've cried out past traumas and cleared my body from pain that was keeping me stuck. I've seen visions of my ancestors and ancient women around the bed. I've purified my own karmic baggage in ways that are even difficult to describe. I've held space for my partners to release their pains and traumas, too.

Can you imagine how your partner might expand and change and heal, seeing you deeply opening in your moment of transformation? How their confidence could shift? How the intimacy between the two of you could deepen? Your relationship overall could bust through onto a whole other level of intimacy and connection.

As with anything, when we bring *depth* and intentionality to an experience, our confidence, our magnetism, and our power in the world shift.

All this being said, you usually want to explore this level of lovemaking with someone you *really* trust. Because when you are surrendering so deeply and opening your channels so much, a *lot* of energy and karmic material are exchanged. And if you don't trust the person or know them that well, this can be intense. As on a physical level, you want to chat about STDs before you make love with someone; and on the emotional, karmic, and spiritual levels, you want to make sure you feel safe to surrender completely.

Once I was dating somebody who was in the middle of a divorce, and I knew on some level that because he was missing his child and feeling guilty about not being with him, I was taking on some of his suffering as we made love. In a meditation one day, as I felt into my deepest heart, I was able to feel just how much space his suffering and pain were taking up in my energy field. It was shocking to me. Through the eye of my subconscious, I saw a giant portal connecting me to the suffering of his soon-to-be ex-wife and of his child, both of whom lived in a faraway country. He was making a decision as to whether to move back there or not. It was *heavy*—and it was not mine. But I was carrying some of that weight for him, because we were having deeply soulful sex and were so connected.

It's not like you can have a psychic look over everyone you make love to (and that would be a subjective opinion anyway!). But you can ask your own intuition and your own inner guidance system: "Is it wise to sleep with this person?" And if the answer is "I don't know," as much as you want to dive in, you can choose to wait until you feel fully *ready* to engage in such a deep way. Which may mean waiting until you know if they are doing their own inner work to clean up their side of the street, whether they have investigated their own wounds and patterns—essentially, whether they are taking good care of themselves physically, emotionally, and spiritually and whether their process feels like a match to yours.

This type of lovemaking mirrors the type of living I'm guiding you into in this book. It is vulnerable. It is risky. It can be painful to open so big and to chance being hurt. But when you are able to go there, it is also where you will experience true sexual alchemy, where your patterns and karma can be laid to rest, where fears dissolve, love replaces hurt in your body, and a sense of liberation can be found. These sexual experiences can be incredibly healing to your self-worth, your self-confidence, your relationship with your body, your voice, and your spirit. They can alchemize your pain into power without doing twenty years of therapy. They can open your heart. Crumble walls. Soften you. And bring massive radiance from within out into the world.

So if it's so wonderful, why isn't everyone having deep and soul-shaking-AF sex? Because it means showing your heart. Your soul. Risking looking dumb. It means facing fears, which is very uncomfortable. It means not running away when you get embarrassed. It means staying open, even when you want to make for the hills.

And frankly, on a practical level, this type of lovemaking probably does not look like the kind of sex you see in porn. You can't control it. You can't forecast what traumas or pains may rise to the surface. You will probably cry—a lot. And laugh, too! And you also have to be *in your body* in order for the magic to happen, not thinking about how you look, or what's coming next, or if you smell weird, or if your partner is happy. Instead you commit to the confronting clarity of the present and experience whatever is truly there.

When you are an awakened (or awakening) being and you show up like this—raw, deep, fiery, powerful some days, soft and surrendered on others—you can feel like a locked and loaded weapon in today's world. If you are claiming this power, one glance from you can shift the vibe of a whole room, cause a marriage to crumble, and change whole lives. Making love from this place to someone casually could be devastating to them if they are not doing their own internal work. It could become completely addicting to them, as they see you now as the vehicle for their awakening. Or else the experience could be such a deep opening that they are flooded with their fears and karma and they run and hide for dear life, not understanding what is happening. So please remember that is the level of game we are playing here. It's profound. It's working with energy, the most powerful energy on the earth, the energy of Creation.

I have experienced all of the above and had to deal with the aftermath. The risks involved with claiming this deep power are another reason many of us may unconsciously play small. Because to show up awakened, with all shades of soft and strong and raw and ecstatic and wise surfacing, means you are showing up as Creation herself, and this is seductive and powerful and also can be terrifying. If people are not ready for this, they may be repelled by you. Though, like scared-looking moths to your bright and fiery flame, some may also see your power and want to take it, circle around it, or dim it. There are times when it's wisest *not* to share this power casually with the world and to reveal the depth of it only in safe containers.

In my naïveté years ago, I experienced the shadow side of opening sexually to people who could not meet me at the same level a few times, which produced stalkerish behavior from them when I said I was no longer interested. At first I blamed myself, very much a cultural norm: "It must be my fault I am getting treated like this." But when I sought the advice of a wise woman, she reminded me, "You must be careful who you share your power with at this point in your journey. Anyone you make love to may become addicted to that feeling of being loved and seen by you. They may feel like they're getting to plug into the Divine Mother's electrical socket each time you make love. Be conscious of your powers and use them wisely."

This is a hard one to remember as you smile at someone in the grocery store: that your power is so epic when it's awakened—as it is when it is not coming from your wound or unconsciousness (it is your practice to be constantly discerning this!)—you may be shooting a bolt of lightning into that person just by smiling at them. So smile wisely and stay in your power, stay in your lane. Use your intuition to know when it's safe to share your light.

If you aren't doing your work on yourself, that smile may also have hooks attached to it. You may think it's a neutral, casual smile, but if you haven't been meditating or doing your self-inquiry and processing work, you may not have the expanded awareness to see that that smile is also saying: "I want to be validated. I want to be seen. I want to be loved. I want to be approved of." And that's when things can get tricky.

I am sure you've gotten an email or text from someone laced with these kinds of hooks. It's kind and loving, but something about it feels icky, like it gives you the heebie-jeebies. You're thinking, "Why does this feel kind of creepy? She's just being nice! When did I get so judgmental?!" But truly you are tapping into your own innate wisdom of discernment. And you are feeling that there is a hook hidden in there, and she's looking for validation or approval or crossing a boundary. As you wake up you will see these things and (mostly) feel them.

THE TRANSFORMATIONAL WORK: RECEIVING AND SACRED SEX

As we practice receiving, experiencing depth, and opening, this chapter's practices may feel like more fun than work. They're soft. They're fluid. So give them the space that they need. Set the time, the container, the mood for this magic to arise, and it will integrate into your life.

Receiving Ritual

Receiving can happen only when we take a rest from giving. When our guard is down. When we stop focusing on trying to get what we want and focus instead on creating the space for it to come. I know this can be a frustrating notion at times: "Stop trying so hard—it'll come when you're not looking!" This means letting go of control, and many of us are taught to be in control of our lives and seek what we want instead of allow it to find us. In my own personal experience, I have received the best friends, jobs, and even this book deal when I least expected them.

What I have discovered, however, is a method for creating the environment for receiving. An environment that is anxiety free, soft, open, and heart centered.

Whenever I have found myself obsessing, "When am I going to hear back about that project?!" or "Why didn't they text me back?" I ask myself, "Am I grasping? Clinging? Craving?" If the answer is a resounding *yes*, then I know I may actually be preventing that person from texting or emailing because I have created a hovering, tense energy around the situation. Instead, I let go of the stories in my head, and I drop into doing my embodiment practice. Now, it's almost like clockwork: the minute I *let go*, my energy releases, I have a little cry, then, *ping!*, I hear the text or email come through. I was energetically blocking it with my tension.

So let's do an experiment and spend a full day in receiving mode. If you're a parent or otherwise super busy, this could feel impossible for you, *but* it doesn't mean stopping what you are doing and just sitting. It means dissolving tension around what you want, which you can do with the baby in tow, at your busy job, or wherever you are.

My friend Gala Darling and I have a ritual we started doing years ago called Magical Mornings, to help us get into the receiving mode daily. This ritual is a conscious turn of the radio dial of your brain toward the channel of receiving. It's simple and may seem obvious, but it also helps greatly.

We will start with this practice and then expand on it.

1   Make a gratitude list—this is like a warm-up for your mind. You don't just hop out of bed and go for a run before stretching first, right? Gratitude is your warm-up. You can do this in your journal or notes app or via a text or voice note with a friend. Write down at least four things you're grateful for, up to as many as you like.

2   Now tell a friend, record a voice note, or write in your journal about your ideal day and your ideal life. You can do this one of two ways. In my opinion there is no one way to create transformation, so please feel into your own heart and do what resonates with you:

    •   Past tense, as if it already happened: "I had an amazing day! I worked out and felt so good after. I talked to my boss, who loved my project..."

- Present tense, as if it's happening now: "I am having a beautiful day. I am being rewarded and praised for my talents at work. I am being held by my delicious lover..."

3 Make a commitment to do this ritual *every morning* for forty days.

Forty days is the amount of time it takes to change a habit, so your habit of not being in receiving mode can shift during this time. Every day you will notice that you begin to dream bigger, become more expansive about the way you see your life and how you play in that space of possibility. Make sure you breathe when you do it, allow your heart to be soft, and don't think of it as checking off things from a busy to-do list—*enjoy it!* This is your casting of a spell, crafting of a vision, and calling in what you want.

Sacred Solo Sex Practice

When we aren't experiencing deep sexual union with another human, it can be tempting to succumb to feelings of lack or a sense of needing someone sexually, as opposed to fulfilling your own desires. Or if you're in a partnership, it's easy to get into a routine around sex that begins to feel stagnant and less than transformative. If you have kids and a busy schedule, sex may be the last thing on your mind.

A few years ago, I decided to get to know my own body very deeply and to discover all the types of orgasms I was capable of. This way, not only would I be able to guide someone else to those places, but I would be able to give myself profoundly nourishing sexual experiences when I wanted. Orgasms can be deeply beneficial psychologically and physically, creating an energetic reset for your system with a big release of the so-called love chemical oxytocin. This creates a softening of a deep part of you.

If we have internalized shame about masturbation, it may take a moment to come to see pleasuring oneself as a *sacred practice*. A way of honoring the body and showing it love. Once I began to look at my body as a sacred vehicle that also had an unknown expiration date, I began to see what a gift it was to have been given it. It felt like a joy and an honor to get to know it as well.

Creating a sacred solo sex practice can be similar to creating a meditation practice in that it takes consistency. It takes time. Safety. Presence. Privacy. Overcoming resistance with breath. Allowing space for feelings to arise, some of which may be quite uncomfortable. And doing it again and again without expecting to have the same experience each time. Each time you do enter this sacred space, you will find new gems. You might stumble upon a pocket of grief or pain and have a huge emotional release. You might find laughter. You might find ways to access yourself that you never thought were possible.

If this is your first foray into this kind of practice, I suggest getting a crystal wand to use as your sacred sex tool and treating it with reverence. (See the website for recommendations.) Wrap it in silk or something lovely and keep it somewhere special.

Here are some suggestions for how to build your own sacred solo sex practice:

1 **Compile a playlist.** Include songs that help you feel connected to yourself and your body. I suggest keeping an element of sacredness here and also choosing music that isn't connected to an ex or an emotional memory. Start fresh and make it at least sixty minutes long.

2 **Create the container.** Do you need to lock a door? Turn on a fan or white noise machine? Do you need to make sure the family

isn't home? Draw a bath? Do what you need so you can feel safe to fully let go and relax into the experience.

3 **Start slow.** Get to know your body for a while before you go deeper. You can massage yourself with oil. You can gaze at yourself in the mirror, seeing your naked body and admiring yourself. You can dance sensually. It's up to you how you explore.

4 **Go deeper.** When the moment feels right to go deeper into this practice, stay connected to your breath. You can use your hands for self-pleasure or, as I mentioned, a crystal wand. Breathe and allow for feelings to arise as you stay awake and aware, fully present to the moment. If it feels too uncomfortable, intrusive, or painful, take it slowly. If you've experienced sexual trauma, then slow down even more and stay connected to your breath, your body, and the room. You can do this by breathing audibly, saying aloud to yourself, "I am safe." Or putting your feet on the floor and rooting down.

5 **Breathe.** I can't say this enough. Breath will make the difference between a conscious moment and an unconscious moment of habit, pattern, or replaying of conditioning. One has the ability to heal; the other is routine. If you find yourself clenching muscles or holding your breath, the healing and opening cannot occur. This blocks all other emotional responses in your body and prevents energy from moving through you freely. But as you breathe through any feelings, be they of discomfort or of bliss, the breath will move these emotions through your body and begin to catalyze change.

6 **Enjoy.** This is not just about racing toward the "goal" of orgasm. It is about opening your energetic channels. Re-establishing the connection between your heart and your womb. Dropping into

the deep wisdom of your cervix, letting go of fear, tension, grief, and anxiety, and tuning into wisdom and healing.

7 **Journal.** After your practice you may want to journal. You can ask yourself: "What came up for me?" You can take note of the feelings that surfaced. If shame or guilt or sadness or any other uncomfortable feelings arose, no need to judge yourself—simply take notes.

8 **Release and close.** If feelings are still lingering, this is a great time to cry, moan, dance, shake, sing, engage in breath work, and allow whatever you released to move through you. This is very important before re-entering the world. Then close the container of your practice intentionally with a bath, shower, clothing change, cup of tea, or some essential oils. Create a transition and take some time before reengaging with the world.

Over time, you will journey to deeper places inside yourself during this practice. This may mean breaking through layers of stuck feelings—grief, sadness, anger—at times. On the other side of this internal space creation is an ocean of possibilities: clarity, bliss, and calm, or perhaps healing insights and deep wisdom that impact your life in major ways.

The simple practices of cultivating awareness, getting to know your body more deeply, letting go of old conditioning, softening into your heart, getting into receiving mode, and making internal space will shift the way you walk into a room. The way you carry yourself. The way you enjoy food. The way you laugh. The way you dance. You'll begin to allow things into your life this way instead of hunting things down. You'll unwind guilt and shame about pleasure and your body, and you'll begin to experience your pleasure as a divine act. A prayer. Something that inspires others to get out of their heads and into *their* bodies. Something that inspires the world to see and feel the beauty of nature instead of destroying it. It starts with you and your ability to face your conditioning and patterning, release past hurts, make internal space, and begin to receive the magic of life around you with a renewed openness and clarity.

It takes practice. It may seem much easier to think about the future or pick at the past than to surrender into the present. There is no controlling what you will find or what will arise from the shadows when you surrender. The love is infinite. The bliss is wild. The layers feel never ending. And, yes, pain and sadness are also there, but they simply work in tandem with the joy. Eventually we stop clinging to one state or another, and we allow them to move through us like flowing waves. We open the doors to all of life. We are afraid of much less because we have examined our fears, and they no longer run our lives from the shadows.

This graduation on your path is truly where the magic begins to multiply. This is where personally I have felt great peace, a sense of calm, and love. And also where I have received great news, press, gifts, unexpected money, surprise love. It's all been there when I have faced the tough parts, let go, come through to the other side, softened, and opened to the present moment.

7

HOW TO UNLEASH YOUR FULLNESS AND FIND YOUR VOICE

I can't keep the wild woman in me hiding for long.
No matter how many peaceful meditations I do, sometimes she is
   out for blood.
She comes out whether I like it or not,
Whether I stuff her in skinny jeans and smile sweetly or
Whether I wear the same outfit four days in a row and don't give a fuck.
She looks at my Google cal, all scheduled hour by hour,
And she laughs—threatens to dump coffee on my computer!
She wants to sleep on the earth!
She wants to make out passionately! She wants to breathe fire!

She isn't afraid to walk in cemeteries alone at night.
She's slept under a tarp in the woods for a week.
She's held a baseball bat in her hand while sleeping by the road at night.
She's held a stick while hitchhiking in Mexico.
Dove under fierce waves until she had no breath left—
But where is she now?

Let me search my Google calendar, Gmail, vitamins, green powder,
   Chase bank account, Facebook. Let me ask Siri. No answers there.

Let me search my blood, my tears, my orgasms, my prayers, my words—
Oh yes!
This is where I will find her.
I will not abandon her.
She is my freedom.

MANY OF US OSCILLATE between two common inherited human patterns of being: the pattern of "I am too much" and the one of "I am not enough." We may either internally judge ourselves for being too big, too weird, too loud, too sexual, too hungry, too horny, too curvy, too opinionated, too messy, or taking up too much space, or we may think we don't do enough, aren't pretty enough, don't have enough to say, don't dress well enough, aren't special enough ... It's an internal dialogue and example of thought patterning that plagues most humans at some point on the journey of life.

These types of internal negatively biased narratives can be so insidious that they become a sneaky underlying motivation in the things we do. It means we may also try to predict how others will react to us. For instance, "Is this dress too much?" may seem like a harmless question, certainly not blatantly self-deprecating or hurtful, but with deeper examination we begin to see it does contain the echo of a constant thread of self-judgment and criticism, perhaps linked to microaggressions against the self, so habitual that we have stopped noticing them. When everything we do is preceded by internal questions of "Is this enough?" or "Is this too much?" we are perpetually in the space of negative self-talk, not claiming our power or accepting the present moment, and cutting ourselves off from love. We are reinforcing that we are not okay as we are.

Sometimes those who struggle with the "I am not enough" story overdo things by dressing wildly, being loud, or overcompensating for a little part that believes we will be lovable only if we have something "important" to share, if we are more talkative, more extroverted, funnier, prettier, more charming, sexier than everyone else. Likewise, sometimes the ones who subtly feel "I am too much" are the ones who may adopt a coy, sweet, kind, shy persona to overcompensate.

The internal narratives and dialogues that we engage with all day, every day, not only form our personalities, but they dictate how we serve the world, how we love, how we speak up, and how we claim our power. These subconscious patterns and shadows may be quite sneaky and take time to detect. No need to take it personally, but what you call the self may be a conglomerate of a unique set of patterns packed in your human form. These patterns come from our lived history and change over time.

Ask yourself: "What are three words people would probably use to describe me?"

Take a breath and feel into these descriptions. Are the first ones that come to mind the most obvious? Do they feel the most true?

Now consider how each of those traits formed. If you said "productive" or "high achieving" or "driven," was it due to a parent telling you, "You can do anything, honey! Put your mind to it!" Or did you have a brother or sister who was always outshining you and whom you competed with?

No need to dive too deep into too much self-analysis here. But as we go about reclaiming our *fullness*, something that lives under the patterns, and as we seek to find our most authentic *voice*, we must investigate why we became who we became, why we are how we are. And this can usually be traced back to our childhoods, where the patterns and habits took deep root in our beings.

I can trace my drive, my focus, and my ability to achieve to my father telling me from a young age that I could accomplish anything, be who I wanted to be, and have a big life. He was an immigrant who wasn't able to go to college and struggled and hustled his whole life in order to give me a good one, and he wanted for me not to have to do the same. He would tell me this before bed when I was a child, and these moments created an imprint in me of needing to be somebody special and achieve something big. They also made me believe that my father would love me more and treat me well if I achieved things. So for me, my overachieving quality was mostly a compensating one, stemming from the belief that "I am not enough to receive love unless I have achieved something of value." This belief is one that I have worked hard to loosen and unwind.

When we are stuck in these "too much" or "not enough" stories, or other stories that collapse us inward, we become too distracted to claim our power and our voices in the world. We get stuck in mental patterns and behaviors that fix these stories in place, so much so that we can't expand forward. We sabotage our access to our innate power without even meaning to.

As you seek personal liberation from these internal narratives, you become unafraid to express the full spectrum of your self, in the present, as a being who is changing from moment to moment, no longer stuck. There is less moderating or curating of the self; instead, there is noticing, breathing, and being. A surrender of the internal struggle. You are no longer seeking to fix, to change, but simply to be, regardless of whatever is present. This is the energy of life itself, the goddess, primal energy, Mother Nature in motion. The energy of volcanoes. Wildfires. Snowfall. Gentle rain. Windstorms. Though constantly changing, there is grace and ease and fullness to the full spectrum of textures nature offers us, and as we are a mirror of nature, born from her, if we surrender we too can embody this range of presence and fullness.

There is freedom in this surrender. A voice that says: "I am all. I do not have to pretend to be anything for anyone. All I need to do is live in the present moment and be 100 percent honest about who I am, here, and now. If I am angry, I will allow it to move through me. If I am happy, I will not hide it. If I am sad, I will feel it like a wave. I will not spew, or blame my changing weather on others, or attach myself to the reality of one moment, clinging to it beyond its passing. I will allow each moment to move through me, as a part of my own expression, evolution, and gift to the world."

Born This Way

As I mentioned, I have always wondered what parts of me were created as defenses, as patterns, as responses to life's traumas, and what parts stemmed from my soul tissue. My deep desire to love and be loved was one of the things I often have inquired about. Once, when I was speaking with my mother about this subject, she pulled out a picture of me at age three wrapped around my first boyfriend. Then another picture of me at age four kissing the neighbor boy, Carlos Manuel, on the cheek. Then a picture of me posing in a bikini with another boy. Then a picture with a hairdo I had cut myself at age five, wearing a T-shirt I had drawn on. A picture of me standing naked on a table at age six. She assured me that she had not taught me wildness or flirting but that I had always been that way. It seemed like this was a part of my spirit, my soul makeup, my karma. This "way" was quickly defined by the world as "too much," creating a lifelong internal narrative and pattern in me.

As a result, my focus for many years was on all the ways in which I was "too much," creating a long line of inquiry about every action I took, word I said, and expression I made. For some people, the focus may have been always on what they *weren't*—the ways in which they felt "not enough."

As I've developed conscious awareness of this internal narrative, I've noticed it in fact exists only in relation to others. On my own, I simply *am*. In the same way, your "not enough–ness" likely exists only in relation to others' ideas, ideals, expectations, desires, and insecurities, too.

Think about it. Who are you when you just *are*? When no one is watching?

These internal stories relating to how we show up in the world will always be mirrored in relationships. Once I had a friend who complained to me that my hair was so wild, it called too much attention to me, and I got more attention than her. *Too much*. My own internal fears. Until I made peace with this story, I kept receiving opportunities in my life to rewrite the narrative, mirrored in many friendships and lovers, such as that one. But once we graduate from a particular narrative, although we may see tendrils of it show up here and there, eventually it stops showing up everywhere. Then, when it occasionally does, we realize our relationship to it has changed, we are no longer triggered, we don't bite the bait, and we move on to the next curriculum in our journey.

All outer reflections from others or projections of other people's ideas and opinions onto you can be viewed as blessings in disguise—if you dare to accept them as such—because they give us an opportunity to reclaim our true nature and see where we are with certain shadow material or patterning. For many, the audacity to claim their beauty, their sexuality, their fullness, and/or their voices can bring about great fear. Will we be rejected if we allow ourselves to be this full? And if so, can we let that be yet another lesson in our path's unfolding?

If parts of us trigger or activate shadows or patterns in others, it is essentially not our business. We seek to avoid causing others suffering, but not at the expense of ourselves, and not by causing ourselves suffering. This is a delicate balance that involves learning and cultivating empathy and compassion while also standing in our own power. If other people project their fears and insecurities onto us, it can shake us, and it can hurt, but that is where our own clarity, the depth of our practice, becomes a beacon reminding us of our central home in the heart.

In my own life, I have a few people I trust to be my clear mirrors, helping me see when I am out of line or blind to a pattern. In order for them to have clarity toward me, they must be clear on their own patterns and biases.

I allow for the expression of *my fullness*, my uncharted expression, in safe spaces with safe people, and I trust my inner guidance that I may discern when I am authentically expressing myself or when I am coming from a pattern or story, or compensating, or needing something. It is a moment-to-moment dance, and it all comes back to finding love in each moment.

Whatever is coming through you is your medicine for the moment. That anger might be *just* the right thing to get you *lit* enough to start that organization or write that petition or stop judging yourself. That joy might be *just* the right thing that inspires people around you in a way you could not predict. Those tears may make space inside you for a new creative flow to come in.

Now, as I allow for the embodiment of the *full spectrum* of me, I allow myself to shift and feel into each moment's nuances. I wear or say or write what feels good when it feels good, with awareness, from awareness. If I find myself wondering, "Is this too much?" then I know I probably need to explore it more deeply. And I also discern when my desire to be boldly expressive may come from the shadow of wanting love or attention or approval. The process of discernment is essential and comes only from being honest with one's self, making mistakes, and, again, lots of contemplation and meditation.

Once I went to a workshop hosted by a renowned tantra author and teacher in Berlin. I had packed only a pair of sparkling gold boots as an exercise of externalizing the internal "too much" narrative; I wanted to see what happened and if I could move through it. I knew that after a few days I would wish I had black boots with me so I could blend in with everyone else. So that people wouldn't be looking at me. But I also knew it would be medicine for my divine nature to allow myself to sparkle, to be bold, like David Bowie, seeing how the inside mirrors the outside and vice versa. So for five whole days I wore those boots.

I began feeling a bit sheepish. I went through security in two different airports wearing the gold boots. I walked through my hotel, into taxis, and along the streets of Berlin, where most people were wearing black and gray, and I was dressed all in white with these gold boots. But by day five, the feeling of standing out had become normal to me. I had adjusted to the level of *being seen* that came with sharing myself in this way. Though I was playing with an externalized internal narrative, they were also just shoes. However, it was a practice that I chose as a symbol of something greater, of liberating myself, of becoming more free, and it worked. In those days of self-liberation, I said *yes* to a beautiful love affair in Berlin that profoundly changed my heart, that I do not think I would have entered into had I not been in a space of eliminating fear.

I share this because similar things may happen anytime you share yourself in your biggest and boldest way. It may feel like an epic stretch at first. It can feel intense. Scary. Naked. Exposed. I am really going to let everybody see my wild side?! My artistic side?! My sexy side?! My silly side?! Whatever edge you are expanding past, it takes courage and strength. It is easy to want to go back to just being whatever makes everybody (including you!) the most comfortable.

The same goes for the "never enough–ness," which often shows up unconsciously as "I must be prettier, or thinner, or cooler, or more successful than others." This perfectionism is not only accepted by society today, it's actually encouraged. Voices of "Do more! Exercise more! Make more money! *Push yourself!*" fill our ears. This gives us an excuse to never accept ourselves as we are and to become numb to moments of joy. The sunshine hitting your face, a child putting their head on your lap, someone telling you how much they admire you . . . all of these are lost, because a part of you is fixated on "But I could do better." And so you miss the magic. You miss the moments of beauty attempting to reach you.

We must catch ourselves when those tired stories sabotage our happiness, our peace, our magic, and our power. We must not let them lead or win. Our lives depend on it. In the moment when life is going beautifully, when you are enjoying something, and you notice that perfectionist voice or "not enough" story popping in, even this noticing is a victory to celebrate. Then the next step is to stop and say, "*No way are you winning!* No way are you going to sabotage my power! My expression! My life!" You get to choose what story you believe. Remember you *are* enough. Find a way to celebrate who you are *today*, before you begin to focus on who you are not. Wear the gold boots. Throw out at least five things on your to-do list. Scream. Roar in the mirror. Get rid of the scale. Or do whatever it is for *you* that allows you to be exactly enough as you are. Yes, you will keep growing and transforming and evolving, but you do not have to postpone your happiness. Right now, you are enough.

How to Say "Fuck It" and Accept Yourself

A glorious reclaiming of your internal battery power comes when you accept who you are now. Whether you feel wildly extroverted at a party and want to laugh loudly and feel like the queen of the room or you want to sit in the corner and just observe, you are at peace. Because you are in alignment with yourself in that moment. To fuck like a goddess means you become one with the present, you make love to the moment, *and* you find a way to love and accept who you are in the moment. Whether you are quiet. Whether you are loud. Whether you are shy. Whether you are silly. Whether you are sad. You show up as *you*. You throw away what "they" told you to be. What you think you "should" be. You emanate your divinity and trust that whatever flavor of divine shine is moving through you at that moment is *perfect*. This is when you and all of Creation are flowing as one. In this moment you emanate life-force. You are a magnet for life's bounty.

How to Express Yourself Fully and Find Your Voice

A huge part of claiming your power is sharing your voice with the world. This could be done in the way you chat and communicate with friends and family, the way you present ideas, the way you share your heart, and the way you offer your unique gifts to the world. The voice is a channel for the divine to move through you via the magic of language. It is a channel for the exchange of culture and ideas, the protection of the earth and its peoples. It's a place where energy moves through you and out into the world.

We all have something to say, whether it's at a dinner party, on social media, in writing, in speaking, or in teaching our children. We can either *speak up* and share from our true power, or we can play safe, shying away from saying anything risky, shying away from telling the truth because it may hurt too much or it may make someone uncomfortable. This is how we maintain the status quo and how things do not evolve.

You find your voice first and foremost by claiming your story—owning what has happened to you. The things you have seen, experienced, endured. The lessons you've learned. Trust me, if you've been through any kind of life lesson or experienced any kind of pain, you have something extremely valuable to say. Whether that lesson came from the pain of stubbing a toe or the pain of facing breast cancer, I guarantee you have a powerful message you can share around it, be it with your family or with the world. "Who, me?" you may be thinking. Yes, *you*.

Have you ever seen a picture of vocal cords? They look *very* vaginal. And there is indeed a physical and also an esoteric connection between the voice and the power within the yoni/vulva/womb and the heart. If you have that in your body, you may look to that mirror as a source of inspiration. In many Eastern traditions it is said that the human body has thousands of inner energetic channels. Our central channel goes straight up the middle, connecting our energy centers, also known as chakras. If the energy is flowing freely and unblocked between those power centers, the magic *flows!* The voice carries the vibes of the deepest parts of you, regardless of your anatomy, and there is immense power in it. And once you start coming online with your truth, healing and sifting through karmic material and living from your fullness and true essence, you will likely want to speak up, shout praises to the heavens, sing, and write and share stories in whatever way suits you.

You claiming your unique voice and story and sharing them with the world—be it over dinners, or in books, or on social media— becomes a gift to everyone around you, a unique medicine for the world that only you can deliver. When you use your voice to express stories, or joy, or anger, or wisdom, it has the power to open hearts, to inspire, and to heal others, too.

One way you could know you're ready to reclaim *your* voice is when you find yourself judging others for being "too loud" or "too opinionated" or you find yourself critical of others in general. During some years of deep healing, I had dived into my serious "spiritual" side and put my silly side away. Such are the phases of life . . . but I missed that part of me. I had fully embodied that side in my spiritual comedy web show, *Be Here Nowish*. It was indeed a part of me, yet it felt far. And then I met Sah. My dear friend, fellow author, and teacher Sah D'Simone is a joyful burst of sunshine of a human. He laughs loudly almost all the time. He dances in the street. And when we went on a three-week pil- grimage to India and Nepal together, I was completely triggered by his constant laughter. I thought, "Okay, come on, it's time to get spiritually *serious* now!" But he just kept on laughing. About everything! After a while I broke down and started laughing too. I shattered my own spiritually serious glass ceiling, and I found laughter and joy *everywhere*. We were on a trip to experience high tantric Buddhist initiations and meditate in secret Nepali caves, and though our own karmic material, wounding, and patterning was brought forth by the deep work we did, my heart could not have been more filled with *joy*. Our act of joyful expression no doubt shifted the hearts and minds of many people we encountered along the way.

For me, the part of my own voice and fullness I had been afraid of was that of joy. For some it may be expressing anger or talking openly about sex. Whatever area we shy away from using our voice in is often the place we are secretly *wanting* and being called to express more fully! Using our voice inspires and gives permission to others to do the same.

THE TRANSFORMATIONAL WORK: CLAIM THE FULL YOU

For our practice in this chapter, we will play with a few ways we can expand into our fullness and use our voices. These are simple things you can do that will *free* you from the limiting stories and allow you to fully own your voice in the world.

Externalize an Internal Narrative Practice

As I illustrated with my story about the gold boots, what I wore was one simple and yet deeply symbolic and external way to practice being too much. If you're thinking, "Oh, that's easy. I don't need to dress in a wild or flashy outfit to prove I'm not too much"—trust me. There is more to this than meets the eye.

Ask yourself: "What constant internal story, judgment, or critique zaps my presence? Is it perfectionism? Too much–ness? Fear of appearing a certain way?"

Take one story, limiting belief, or narrative and find a way to externalize its medicine as I did. Your external expression can be a potent mirror of your internal self. We get to experience this in subtle and not-so-subtle ways.

In this exercise we're going to take a whole week to push your edges of comfort around your *external* expression and see how this helps your *internal* world shift.

Each day this week, I want you to practice negating the story you tell yourself. Do something that pushes an edge only you can define. For example: if you are a perfectionist, allow yourself a week of looking imperfect—perhaps not wearing makeup or not shaving. Pick something that feels outside of your comfort zone but not so distracting that you won't get anything done all week.

When you first try it, take some time to sit with how it feels. Calibrate your system to the state of being slightly outside your comfort zone *externally*. If you've been doing the work in this book, well, then, you've already mastered being outside your comfort zone *internally*, and this may feel like a breeze. Still, take your time with it. You are bringing your external and internal worlds into union. To take a small step before you leap, you may also want to practice at home or in a safe space before you leave the house.

At the end of each day, whip out your journal and write about what you've noticed:

- What was the hardest part of the practice?

- What was the most fun part?

- When did I feel silly or small and why?

- When did I feel empowered?

- Was there any feedback from others, and if so, what did they say?

Then, at the end of the week, notice how your experiment progressed: Did you expand into being more radically self-expressed and free? Or did you feel awkward and shy? Either is *okay*. There is no right or wrong.

You can repeat this exercise for as many weeks as you want, testing the waters with different levels of comfort-zone expansion and externalizing different internal narratives. For example, if you find yourself constantly criticizing how weak or how shy you are, spend a week being the opposite and make choices and plans to support that practice.

Remember, who we are *externally* is a mirror of our internal state, so the purpose of this exercise is to pave the way for your inner shine to radiate outward and for you to experience what is holding you back. Pay close attention. The nuances in the internal shifts can be subtle but powerful.

The Let Yourself Be, Not Do, Practice

Now, you can allow the *exact* opposite and practice being and not doing with these internal narratives. Instead of course correcting constantly, or obsessing, or acting out your internal stories, pick a narrative you're working with—a big one—and just let it be for this week. In the moments when the chatter floods into your mind, you will get the choice to relax and allow yourself to simply *be* "not enough" or "too much" or "imperfect" instead of continuing to pick on yourself. Treat it like you are on vacation from that internal struggle this week. And when it comes up, refocus your energy away from fixing or figuring out and toward something else.

Take inventory of what behaviors you need to refrain from in order to be on vacay from this narrative. Perhaps there are people you need to take a break from this week.

You will have the opportunity to begin to rewrite the story. Journal and notice what comes up, how hard or easy this practice is, when you are able to stick with it and when you can't. Praise yourself for the moments you are able to let this story be—every moment, or minute, or hour is worth celebrating.

Find Your Voice Practice

Now that you've excavated and cleared some of the key internal stories that are keeping you from sharing, speaking, and being seen, you can begin to claim your voice. To share it openly! Freely! Without worrying what anybody else will think. This external expression is the natural progression of all the inner work we have done so far, and I am so excited for you! Now it is time to *do it*. The "too much" and "not enough" stories are just two main ones that prevent us from using our voices. But there are *many* others. Some others that I love are: I'm too busy, don't have the money, not ready, too stressed, need to plan more, need to do more work. We have a hundred excuses why we don't claim our power and our voices in the world. But I know you are now smart enough not to buy into any of that fake news anymore!

For this exercise, let's set some intentions that you can practice out in the world. If you forget these, you can always come back and read them again.

First, write down a few ways you are ready to own your voice. For example:

- I promise to speak up at work next week when I don't agree with something, even if I am the only one with a different opinion.

- I promise to tell my partner when my feelings are hurt, even if it risks me looking oversensitive.

- I promise to voice my boundaries around my family, even if it upsets them.

Then revisit these things daily as reminders of the new way your voice will move through you, as your commitment to expressing the full, true *you*. Say them in the mirror. Text them to a friend. And then actually do them!

Remember, when it comes to speaking your *divine truth*, you can take this as *far* as you want! In order to truly free the wholeness of your voice, it will also help to practice:

- Laughing loudly
- Giving compliments to people
- Sharing your opinions
- Telling someone you love them
- Having an extraloud orgasm, solo or with a partner

At first you may feel like you are acting a role, and that is *okay*. The old "fake it 'til you make it" adage is rooted in some truth. But I would like to reframe "faking it" as "practicing it." You are stretching your capacity to *be* a person who speaks up in real time, who shares your truth deeply even when it may feel uncomfortable, and for a while, yes, doing it may feel fake. But try it anyway. Soon enough, embodying this level of self-expression may begin to feel amazing and sexy.

Remember, if you don't do this, you run the risk of staying small or staying quiet in situations that are *not okay*. The risk of not being the epic, legendary, *true you*.

Got it?

You deserve to have a legendary laugh.

You deserve to have a legendary look.

You deserve to have a legendary orgasm.

You deserve to say "No."

You deserve to have an opinion on the world.

You deserve to be someone whom others are inspired to be like!

It takes practice. But using your voice may inspire people in ways you cannot predict. It may bring courage into a room. Bring healing to peoples who haven't had a voice. You using your voice and risking it being "too much" or "not enough" just may be the exact medicine that the world needs. Will you hold all that back? Or give it freely? The world needs you now more than ever. Not to mention that it can feel so good to scream, to shout, to sing, to write poetry, to tell stories. It feels better than all the sweets, the TV shows—all of it. It's embodied. It's alive. It's human. And it is yours. The voices that have been dominating this planet and dictating so much of what happens have been in power long enough. It's time for us all to rise. To listen. To speak. To bring forth the stories that have been buried deep and hold them up like banners! To unearth the truth. The things that have happened and are hiding out in hearts. To scream them, cry them, and mourn them together. This life is yours to claim. Speak up. The world needs you.

8

FUCK LIKE A GODDESS NO MATTER WHAT LIFE BRINGS YOU

I am willing to risk comfort, security, and safety in order to
   claim my magic
Because my magic is not always to be found in obvious,
   comfortable places.
It's deep in my inner caves.
It requires risks. It requires missions to the moon.
It requires walks out of tune.

I tried looking for my
Special flavor of magic in the mall,
On Amazon Prime, in copies of *Vogue*,
In a certain size. A certain look.
But my magic is way too crafty to be found there.
It's not found in the obvious.
It requires a jump off a cliff to find.
It requires a walk in the dark.
It requires a bit of blood,
Tons of tears. Laughs into eternity and things words cannot point to.

I am willing to keep risking comfort
In order to keep uncovering this massive magic of mine.
Take risks,
Defy conventions,
And forfeit approval in order to pave new paths and find this
Magic.

BY NOW YOU'VE EXAMINED your stories with sex, with your body, with love, with your voice and self-expression. You've begun to deprogram your mind and learned how to transmute your feelings and use them as magical nectar for your self-transformation. You've looked at your self-expression and learned how to claim your voice. First off, *congrats*! All this is *huge*! And know that the work will keep working you even after you are done with this book.

Now it is up to you to believe that you can fuck life, make love to your reality, like a goddess *no matter what*. To love and work like a divine radiant being, no matter what shit is going down. On good hair days and bad. Through times of debt and of heart-wrenching breakups. I want you to discover that it is completely within your power to have a wonderful, *powerful* existence every fucking day.

Whether you are broke, sick, angry, or alone, our work together has all been in service of giving you the ability to choose a different story in each and every moment. To embody truth. To embody love. To embody fire. Regardless of whatever external circumstances are presenting in your life!

You've read about people who live this way. A person with no legs running a marathon; a five-time cancer survivor building a home for kids; a woman who survived genital mutilation and rape going on to help educate little girls. Or maybe you see examples in your own life: a friend who went on a retreat mid-breakdown and returned a new person; someone who had the courage and vulnerability to share their abuse story online; or the family member who overcame depression and now shines *really* bright. The people who have said, "Fuck it. I am going to become bigger and shine brighter than the shit life has thrown at me!"

When you can say this, you are no longer letting the external dictate your experience of your life. And this is when you begin to come into sacred union with your own divinity.

By this stage in your life, you will likely have heard enough people tell you, "Oh, life is so *hard*!" It's also highly likely that you have bought into this story. Whether you've been broke, sick, divorced, there will have been plenty of evidence to confirm that, "Yep, life sucks!!!"

And yes, life will undoubtedly bring traumas and dramas and sickness and heartache. But we can also allow these things to be the catalysts for our internal transformation, to move through us, carving depth into our insides, without breaking us. It is fully within our power to stand up, to share, and to love big, even when it hurts. To dance, even in grief. To sing through the tears. To not shut down, or numb out, or pretend it's all okay. To extend a hand to others in pain, even when we are still nursing our own wounds.

When those woes arrive, we can choose to be a victim, to get torn down, and to let the old stories creep in. "See!" the stories will say. "I told you that you'll never find true love!" Or "You knew the fun was bound to end!" Or we can find a way to make *art* out of the pain, letting it move through our systems with breath and tears and pen on paper, and rewrite the narrative. One that perhaps our mothers didn't get to choose. Or our grandmas. Either you let the fear voices *win* and keep you small, or you choose a new story.

The fear will come. Remember, it's just trying to keep you safe. But I'm here to say: *You don't have to let the fear run your life.* You are done with that. You have your toolkit. You know what to do in case of a fear emergency. This is when you work *with* your shadow, you love on your child self, you stay awake and aware, and you don't hide from the fear. It's when you use your breath and the power of writing, of cultivating awareness, and of letting fear open you up more instead of keep you small. You know how to speak up and confront your fear head on. It's the moment when, truly, the only way out is through the dark tunnel between the old parts of you and the new ones, with its creepy-crawlies and glowing doors. It's the epic journey of you. It's scary at times, yes. But there is also so much magic in your mysterious unfolding.

This means being dedicated to your uncovering, your blossoming, to finding the diamonds in your heart and soul, above all else. So you can make *love* to everything in your life like the divine powerhouse that you are. Give your gifts to the world before you die. Share your love, your heart, your voice, your laugh. Letting it all be the medicine that the world needs. Trusting it is needed. You are needed. You are here for a reason.

When you allow life to move through you with ease, even in the face of adversity, there is no separation between you and your laugh and the sun and the way you move. You are living in divine union with everything around you, and it is evident in how you speak, eat, walk, scream, cry, love. All that you do becomes an embodiment of the divine energy.

I want to guide you toward this epic reclaiming of your power, so you can truly make love to life, to yourself, to your passions, and to your work and also so you can heighten the way you enjoy your food, the clothes you choose to wear, and the people you choose to have in your life. It is essentially your choice how you dance the dance of your life and how you leave any inherited and subconscious blocks behind once and for all.

Let this be a final reminder that you deserve to walk through the world with a bounce in your step and your internal battery full of juice and *power*, excited to fuck and be fucked by life in a consensual, exciting, loving, and magical way—*no matter what*.

How Not to Give a Fuck about the Stupid Stuff

The present moment is the only place from where we can become aware, go against our conditioning, and make a different choice, one that is truly aligned with and in the flow of love.

When our minds are busy reliving the past or tripping into the future, we miss the world making love to us *now*, asking us to dance with it, moment to moment. We miss the songs that are playing in the grocery store *just for us*. A kid smiling at us. Someone complimenting us. You are not available for any of this, and your radiance and magnetism are on hold, waiting for you to drop back into the present, where the universe is ready to make love to you.

What I mean is that it's ready with business ideas, wonderful orgasms, creativity, laughter, and boundless joy! As well as love. It wants to come into sacred union with you.

Of course, the present moment is also where the big stuff happens: the breakups and the illnesses. We can't discount that and the intensity they bring. Yet it's often the stupid stuff that keeps us in a constant struggle, the little annoyances and so forth that can derail our happiness if we let them. But if we surrender to the divine flow of it all, we can often receive a *present*—meaning we can come to see the gift in it all.

How to Transform the Big Stuff into
Fuel for Our Awakening

Many of my clients have been through multiple traumas, and I have learned from working with them, and from my own journey, that it's no easy feat to move past these, integrate them, and see them for the gold they've given us so we can feel good and shine in the world. "Wait, you want me to be surrendered in the present moment?! Life doesn't feel safe!" But when we work on using breath and sound and getting into the body, letting the pain carve out space and massage out the insides, something magical happens. It's like a layer of muck gets scrubbed off. The pain opens us, deepens us, and allows us to rise into a new space in life, like a phoenix—if we can be brave enough to show up to the fire.

This is how we make love to the present. By letting it truly fuck you, in "good" and "bad" ways. When we try to manipulate life to only give us the "good" times (which are based on our subjective experience of "good"), then we cannot grow, because we are running from the discomfort that is actually there to teach us, to open us, and to level us up! When we turn toward the discomfort, the present moment becomes our personal trainer, making us stronger and more powerful by delivering the life lessons we need in order to evolve.

This frame is a way to define the path of the modern spiritual being, the visionary, the tantrika, the priestess, the alchemist—whatever term resonates with *your* path. It is to declare, "I am going to surrender to the present. I am going to dive into the lessons of Earth School. I am going to stop avoiding pain or fear or discomfort and allow myself to grow and know myself more, know the divine more, and know love more. This life is a gift to my awakening! I want to wake up. I want to remember my true nature. And I will not shy away from doing so. For the benefit of all beings!" You stop fearing whether people like you or not, you stop fearing rejection, and you stop fearing life. You allow it all to open you. To teach you. To empower you. To turn you *on*, the good and the bad. And with all that fear gone, there is space in your body and your life for the *light* to get in. For magic. For truth.

"A women unafraid of her shadows radiates light." This phrase came to me while I was on a Buddhist retreat learning a dakini practice with a high lama, or teacher, learning to sit even deeper in my own shadows so that I could make space for more light. It was clear to me that in the society we live in, where we focus on getting light from the outside—by applying shiny makeup and putting diamonds in our ears—what we are really doing is hiding from the things that are preventing our *own* light to shine: our shadows, the conversations we don't want to have, the relationships we are afraid to walk away from, the habits we know deep down are not good for us.

When we commit to being *all in* with life, to letting each moment open us, play with us, seduce us, shock us, tease us, kiss us, and caress us, we begin to radiate light from within. It is when you are becoming one with the moment and fucking it, surrendering to it, letting it open you, teach you, bring you to bliss's edge, and detonate you all at the same time.

How to Surrender and Fall into the Magical Flow of Existence

An essential part of discovering how to fuck like a goddess is learning to surrender control.

Imagine a sparkling woman walking down the street. Everyone's heads are turning to watch her. She embodies something magical, something radiant; she is freedom in motion! What she looks like doesn't matter. Her clothing doesn't matter. She just radiates light. WTF!? How can this be??! What is her secret?!

She trusts life.

She is at ease.

She is surrendered to life's flow.

She has made peace with life, and they are now in cahoots.

Now imagine the same woman, but she's checking her phone again and again. She's looking around to see if people are noticing her. She's adjusting her dress. She's watching her reflection in all the shop windows to see if her hair is in place. Is she magnetic? Is she radiant?

Perhaps, but she is clearly *not* trusting the flow of life to hold her. Maybe she doesn't quite believe she's worthy of being held, or perhaps part of her is stuck in the past, afraid something will happen like before and she will get hurt again. Her beautiful heart is in there, and maybe we see glimpses of it, but she is not at ease with life's flow.

Let's be real: this may be most of us, most of the time, and that is okay. We are all learning, together, as a collective. Because it takes *tons* of faith to simply trust life and the present moment. After all, many of us have been through some *intense* shit. If you are tense, anxious, and/or living with PTSD as a result, then the surrender practice I'm about to describe may be *much* harder for you. And that is *okay*. I've been through some epic stuff, and so have many of the women I have worked with, and if we can do it, so can you! Because what is the other option? To never allow yourself to feel held by your life? To never allow yourself to feel free? You deserve to be that radiant being walking down the street, totally trusting all that is.

Surrendering to life, to nature, and to the greater flow is the opposite of what the patriarchy has taught us. It has tried to control time.

Nature. Our bodies. And the art of surrendering to the magic that is beyond explanation, that same magic that makes flowers blossom and shooting stars pop through the air—that art is not taught in geometry classes or history classes about wars and economics. We are taught linear thinking. We are taught to seek certainty. To think in formulas. So to stop and say, "Fuck that! I am going to surrender to something bigger than me" is a *revolutionary* thing to do! When conflicts arise in our lives, instead of attempting to *do* more, to *fix*, to handle, to control, what if we stopped and breathed and let go a little bit? Surrendered to divine grace? To the magic that is beyond what we can see? Some other cultures have nailed this. It's beautiful. It makes me drop to my knees and kiss the earth with tears falling.

It is possible for all of us. Yes, we have a lot of dismantling of systems to go, but it's happening as each one of us is healing, standing in our power, and reclaiming our voice.

Remember: you are *so* much stronger than you think. You've fallen before and picked yourself up and started again. Which means that should you surrender and, in the worst-case scenario, fall, you know you can put yourself back together again, right? So why not just risk it? Not blindly, but with awareness. With clear intention. With presence. Walking through life like a queen who knows what she is doing. Who has made the sun, the moon, the trees, the rain, and the birds her allies in this life. Who loves to love. Who loves to *live*. And who is unafraid of her hurt, her anger, and her sadness and therefore unafraid of being exactly who she is in any given moment.

On my Surrender Saturdays, I follow my inner guidance system, not the clock. I take time to rest, to lie and look out the window, to bask in the sun, to dance, to play, to allow my day to unfold in a totally unstructured way. And in this, I practice the art of surrender. The art of *being* versus *doing*.

Your own surrender practice could be as simple as leaving your phone at home and wandering through your neighborhood, going into a cafe for a tea, reading a book, picking some flowers. Or it could mean doing a two-hour meditation and breath work practice where all your channels open so wide that you hear the voice of the divine coming through you.

But practice the art of surrender you must, or you will continue to be a slave to to-do lists, Google cal invites, and iPhone notifications. And you may miss life's magic flowing through you.

Even if you live only one day a week this way, it will change your whole vibe. More sexy juiciness will ooze up and through you. More ease will emanate from you. People will feel good being around you, because you will be reminding them it's okay to trust yourself and be with the flow.

It also can be fifteen minutes of surrender with breath. It doesn't have to be a whole day. You find a way to be in that feeling of free-falling. Of swimming naked in the ocean. Of dancing with wild abandon. *In the here and now.*

And you'll be making love to life, fucking like a goddess, naturally, with ease and grace.

THE TRANSFORMATIONAL WORK: FUCK LIKE A GODDESS TIME

How to let go, how to surrender, how to make space for the magic that lives in you to come out? It can only happen through practice! In the final part of our work together, I will share some of my favorite ways to do this.

Surrender Practice

Get your journal out, and let's take a moment to consider where you are *great* at surrendering and also where you may need a little help.

When is the last time you felt totally at ease? When things just flowed, and while you put some effort in, you didn't *struggle* or *push*. Write about that day in your journal. Maybe it was on your last vacation or your last day off. If you can't seem to remember a day, choose a single moment. Perhaps post orgasm. After a yoga class. A moment when your whole self felt loose, relaxed, and at ease.

Now ask yourself:

- How did that day feel in your body?
- Did you experience anger that day?
- Did you get bored?
- What moments do you remember most?

Next, I want you to consider your week. How many moments like this do you usually have? Come up with a percentage of time when you feel surrendered and free versus scheduled, driven, and focused. How much of your week is spent in the space of *surrender*?

These can be little moments: for example, "Wow, after each shower I generally walk around naked, singing and dancing and laughing for at least thirty minutes, and I feel totally free, and I do that *at least* three days a week." They don't have to be anything groundbreaking.

But I want you to become aware of them so that you can *prioritize* them—because these small moments of surrender have the power to totally shift your presence from *go go go* and *do do do* mode to simply *being*. In Italian there is a phrase you may have heard, *dolce far niente*: "the sweetness of doing nothing." And yes, this is a foreign concept to many of us! The act of *being* without *doing* something is very hard for the modern human. We're often trying to do at least three things at once. We're on the treadmill while listening to a podcast and also texting a friend. There *is* something badass about that level of multitasking, but also, if we don't watch it, that level of *doing* can make our hearts hard, our intuition less clear, and our yonis less sensitive.

Once you've begun to notice the places you feel this free and open to the flow, then it's up to you to add more of them to your life. To prioritize them. To *choose* them instead of opting for the things that cause anxiety and cramp your flow.

Craft Your Surrender Saturday or Microsurrender Time

As I shared, it can be super helpful to schedule one day per week for surrender, to allow the divine in you to emerge and to speak. This might sound like an oxymoron, to schedule this meeting with divinity, but as with any healing practice, this is about creating a *container* for it to happen in! I like using my Saturdays this way, but if that doesn't work for you, then choose another day, and you can also just commit to one day each month. If you're a busy mama and you can commit to just ten minutes of wildly dancing naked or however you want to surrender, that too is *great*.

Start by making your own guidelines that you know bring you a sense of surrender. I look at this time as one of entering into my goddess temple, my priestess cave, my space of inner visioning, of listening, of reconnecting. It feels ancient once I get in there. It also feels essential. Like, how did I forget how important this is?! It's a special space that appears only when the noise is quieted.

Here are a few of my favorite ways to access this magical inner surrender temple:

- **Phone on airplane mode or do not disturb.** Nothing gets me out of juicy surrendered goddess mode like three texts from my dad and a Chase banking alert. *No, thank you.* I deserve a few hours a week undisturbed.

- **A long embodiment practice.** I begin my day using my own recording (the same one I mentioned in chapter 3, which you can access on my website), which I listen to lying on the floor, nested in blankets. If by the end I haven't had a good cry, or laugh, or growl, then I know I may not have broken through the surface thoughts in my mind. If my heart and yoni have yet to speak to me, then I keep going until they do.

- **Time to write.** I put on the *best* playlist, and I get a delicious oat milk latte or cup of tea, and I write my little heart out. As if I was Anaïs Nin or Henry Miller or D. H. Lawrence or Rumi. I let myself be as *free*, as mystical, as sexual, and as weird as I want, and I just *write*.

Also: Nudity. Wild hair. Orgasms. Fruit dripping down my chin. No undies. Laughter. Loud music. Poetry. Waterfalls. Cold showers. Salt baths. Make your list! Remember what enlivens and awakens you to your own sense of surrender!

Sometimes I may add a heart-opening cacao elixir or some music that induces trance vibes. You can use breath work or herbs or dance or song or drumming to enter into altered states if you like. You can take it as far out as you wish!

Then, once I'm in the zone, some of my Surrender Saturday practices include:

- Cooking up a huge stew while wearing a beautiful flowing dress and singing along to Nina Simone

- Taking a luxurious bath with rose petals floating in it and *alllll* the oils

- Getting a massage

- Giving myself a long and slow self-pleasure practice

- Lying in the sun on the beach or on my carpet at home and just staring into space

It's up to you how you create the conditions for the divine flow to come and to open you so that you can feel the juicy connection between your body, your heart, and your soul and let it be *bigger* than the mind's games. Bigger than the conditioning! Than the fears! In order to surrender to this internal voice of true *flow*, we must feel safe, so make your nest and do what you need to do to create that safety. When your system is in fear, you won't be able to let go. When cultivating a surrender practice of your own, finding a safe space to vision, to listen, to dream, and to let go is essential.

9

CONCLUSION | WHY I HAVE COMMITTED TO A LIFE OF SURRENDER

THE REINS OF CONTROL and the to-do lists and goals have been on the forefront of my mind most of this life. The idea of getting somewhere, being something. The notion that I could lie back and let some things come to me while pursuing others with ease, that I could live with an open heart and not also be watching over myself, seemed crazy to me. Yes, I saw evidence of people who seemed to be embodying a deep sense of openhearted trust, despite the odds. But it seemed easier to have a plan. Make sense of life. To "*know*" things. To admit to not knowing, to not having a formula or a plan—that seemed dumb and scary. Yet somewhere deep inside I knew that was the key. That the most glorious moments of love and bliss I have experienced in this life have happened when I let go. When I stopped pushing. When I allowed the fire in me to rise. When I said yes. When I let myself be fucked open by life and the moment, instead of being stuck in my head, thinking about my plans or my looks or my fears.

I figured, the divine does a great job at making flowers blossom and babies be born. Maybe I should let go of some of my agendas and surrender to the divine? To ask in the morning: How can I give today? How can I show up? How can I soften to this life? See the mystery in it and *revel* in its magic, instead of being stuck in my thoughts? I know how good it feels to be in the *flow*. And I am committed to that life of letting go and letting god, goddess, divine flow, source be at the *heart* of me, instead of fear and worry and anxiety and lists and boxes. Opening my heart to the moment, again and again and again, instead of closing it off and going into my head.

The thing I learned is that there is no formula, no guarantee, except committing to the present. To loving with an open heart. To feeling. To breathing. To letting *every* moment be a sacred moment of awakening, versus letting moments pass as mundane and casual, as if I were asleep. I choose *awake*. That means showing up so deeply, so alive, and so unattached to outcomes that it can be fucking scary.

When you fuck like a goddess, the stakes are high. It can be frightening. You risk looking dumb or not knowing what will happen. But you risk for love. For living. For waking up. You do it, not only for you, but for the planet, the beings who will meet you with your wide-open, raw heart and light shining through your eyes. Who will hear your screams and cries protecting the earth, your laughter shuddering through the skies. Who will witness your orgasms like a healing balm on the atmosphere.

You will want to run at times from this level of openhearted living. It's like sitting in the fire some days. Burning at the stake. I am not gonna lie. It can hurt to feel all the feels. I try to run all the time! I tried to run from this book. Because I knew I had to be open and vulnerable, and I knew it would hurt to open my heart so wide and get so real. I can't fake it. I can't wrap life up in a bow and say, "Here is how to do it." But I can remind you that you have everything you need to do this. To love big. To share your voice! To stand in your massive power! To have the uncomfortable conversations. To hold the hands of someone you hurt and kiss them. To see the injustices and feel them and take a stand. To be a light in a world where the decisions being made are awful at times. We need your voice. Your heart. *Alive and open.* Raw! Bloody! Messy! Full of joy and sadness and vitality, inspiring others to come out from behind the screens and hug each other and connect and love and be vulnerable and mourn and grieve for what is happening here. For the destruction. For the birth. The death. And everything in between. And from there we keep opening and evolving into the next level of being on this planet. A level where perhaps we are more divine and less human. More in love and less in fear. Making more moments of dancing and less war. Doing more planting and less cutting down.

It starts here. *Now.* In this moment of you showing up to life, fucking it deeply, letting yourself be fucked open wide and tall and broad and stretched. This is your expansion. The next level of *you* fucking like a goddess or god or fairy or warrior or light being or whatever you want to *fuck* and be fucked as. *Fucking* is divine communion with the present. Saying, "I am here! Let's be together, you and me, present moment! I am *yours.*"

It's a glorious surrender to lie down and open to the present moment, inviting it in like a lover you don't want to look away from. This is it.

Enjoy it. The hair pulling from life. The spankings. And the tears that drip from your eyes in gratitude for the ecstasy at hand.

The moment is yours. Make love to it.

I dare you.

ACKNOWLEDGMENTS

THIS BOOK IS INSPIRED BY all the people out there who have the courage to heal, to change the paradigm, and to shatter illusions about our bodies, our sexuality, our spiritual selves, and the nature of our minds. You Bright Bold Brave Spirits forging the new dawn on this planet, fuck yeah. I honor you deeply for being walking reminders of the Divine Wow that we all have tucked in our hearts, even in a world that can feel as dark as it is light. Through your bravery I have been reminded to never give up on waking up.

It is by the grace of all those writers and artists and visionaries and teachers who have walked before me that I have the courage to raise a voice, to speak, to share, to question, to grieve, to feel, to make art—as imperfect, messy, and ever changing as I am. This book is a combination of the poetry of my soul, the ideas in my mind, the blood in my heart, the scars on my body, and the light in my eyes. My hope is that it helps someone else on their journey, and for me that is enough.

I have tremendous gratitude to everyone who has played an essential part in my own healing and awakening journey thus far. Thank you to those people who reflected to me my shadows and helped me wake up. Thank you to the people who have been the bearers of the tough lessons for my soul. Thank you to those who have held me when I was at my lowest and celebrated me when I was at my highest.

Thank you to my mother, Cynthia, who has been the great teacher and greatest support of my life. A spirit whom I've been to hell and back with, whom I will be high-fiving in the next dimension for this life's karmic breakthroughs together. Who has shown me love and forgiveness and support for my own awakening all these years, deciphered my voice through choking sobs on long-distance phone calls, made me laugh, and held me unconditionally. Thank you to my father, John Paul, for being one of the greatest teachers of unconditional love and of self-love, adventure, wildness, romance, and pain. The love and depth I have learned from this relationship surpasses my wildest dreams. Gratitude to both my parents for allowing me to share their stories with such generosity.

And to my soul family. Rebecca. Shannon. Vikain. Ruby. Moun. Sah. Daniel. Daniella. Knomia. Lisa. Paul. Erica. And many others. You all have held me in the deepest ways. Taught me how to love and be loved. Forgiven me when I was asleep and received me in all iterations. You are my teachers, my family, my heart.

Thank you for the wisdom and sharing of the spiritual teachers and mentors who have changed my life: Bobby Drinnon, Starhawk, David Deida, Deborah Kampmeier, Lisa Levine, Lama Tsultrim Allione, Ram Dass, Betsy Bergstrom, Sally Kempton, and everyone at NYU and the Stella Adler Studio of Acting.

And to my great plant teachers, ayahuasca and mushrooms, and the peoples and cultures who have shared these treasures with me: Thank you for awakening me to my true nature again and again and again, giving me the toughest love, showing me where I am strong and where I have work to do, and allowing me to see more of the greater picture and nature of the cosmos. Thank you for teaching me the nature of love.

Thank you to my spirit teachers, Michael, Odin, Mother Mary, Yeshua, Mary Magdalene, Kali, Krishna, Radha, Shiva, Guru Rinpoche, Chögyam Trungpa Rinpoche, Ram Dass, Amma, Yogananda, Anandamayi Ma, and all the other deities and masters who visit me from all the past incarnations and allow me to embody their qualities through my form. To the lineages that carry the wisdom that has awakened me from my dark nights of the soul and provided me a road map home.

Thank you to the team behind this book—my agent, Marilyn, and my editor, Diana—for believing in me and holding me when I wobbled and quaked in fear. And to Ruby for helping me make sense of my ideas. Thank you! To the team at Kripalu, to Ellen Rose, for bringing the wild and weird ladies into that place. I am so grateful.

And to Sabrina, who has been the grounded earth in my life as the manager of my business, giving me space to soar, to dream, to create. Staying calm when I seek to create and destroy, when I become soft and when I become pure fire. I thank you from the bottom of my heart.

Above all, thank you to the divine spark that lives in me, that seems to be crazy enough to speak, to share, to live, to dream, to make mistakes, and to keep waking up. You Wild Flame of Eternity and Love, bless you for gracing my human existence.

ABOUT THE AUTHOR

ALEXANDRA ROXO is a spiritual teacher, artist, and writer specializing in the art of self-healing, transformation, and feminine embodiment. Her writing and views on personal growth, healing, the divine feminine resurgence, and modern spirituality can be read on the websites of *Playboy*, *Vogue*, and mindbodygreen. She has been featured in many publications for her deep, sensual, and raw approach to healing and transformation and has been named a "modern spiritual leader" by Well+Good. She has also appeared on multiple TV shows, such as *Slutever* on Viceland and *Sex Life* on Epix, and has been featured in top podcasts.

Her work as a filmmaker and on-camera host took her to Cuba to shoot with the Castro family, to a truck-stop strip club in New Mexico, and to favelas in Brazil. Her feature film, *Mary Marie*, was well reviewed in *Variety* and bought by TLA Releasing in 2013. Her Vice documentary, *Every Woman* (2014), has been viewed by more than 12 million people online. Her highly acclaimed web show, *Be Here Nowish*, was featured in press ranging from the *New Yorker* to *Vogue* and touted as "the new New Age" in the *Times* of London. Her feature film script, *One for the Road*, was selected for the Independent Film Project and the Film Society of Lincoln Center's Independent Film Week and the Tribeca Film Festival labs, as well as being a Sundance Institute Screenwriters Lab finalist. She has also directed and hosted branded content and commercial work for many companies over the years. All her film work can be found online through Vice, Ora TV, YouTube, and Amazon. In addition, Alexandra has taught writing and art workshops at homeless shelters and through NGOs, with a focus on helping women express themselves through artistic means.

Alexandra has spent her adult life pursuing her healing and studying sacred plant medicines, shamanism, sacred intimacy work, and tantric Tibetan Buddhism. She currently divides her time between several pursuits. She spends time monthly on retreat and in study, apprenticeship, and nourishment with internationally acclaimed teachers and plant master teachers. When she is in Los Angeles or New York she is in service, teaching clients and students, writing content, and visioning and creating new projects, or she is refilling her cup, dancing, and giving and receiving love with her soul family.

ABOUT SOUNDS TRUE

SOUNDS TRUE is a multimedia publisher whose mission is to inspire and support personal transformation and spiritual awakening. Founded in 1985 and located in Boulder, Colorado, we work with many of the leading spiritual teachers, thinkers, healers, and visionary artists of our time. We strive with every title to preserve the essential "living wisdom" of the author or artist. It is our goal to create products that not only provide information to a reader or listener but also embody the quality of a wisdom transmission.

For those seeking genuine transformation, Sounds True is your trusted partner. At SoundsTrue.com you will find a wealth of free resources to support your journey, including exclusive weekly audio interviews, free downloads, interactive learning tools, and other special savings on all our titles.

To learn more, please visit SoundsTrue.com/freegifts or call us toll-free at 800.333.9185.